The Image of the Prostitute
in Modern Literature

The Image
of the Prostitute
in
Modern Literature

Edited by
PIERRE L. HORN and MARY BETH PRINGLE

FREDERICK UNGAR PUBLISHING CO.
New York

Copyright © 1984 by Frederick Ungar Publishing Co., Inc.
Printed in the United States of America
Design by Jeremiah B. Lighter

Library of Congress Cataloging in Publication Data
Main entry under title:

The Image of the prostitute in modern literature.

   Bibliography: p.
   1. Literature, Modern—19th century—History and
criticism—Addresses, essays, lectures. 2. Literature,
Modern—20th century—History and criticism—Addresses,
essays, lectures. 3. Prostitutes in literature—Ad-
dresses, essays, lectures. I. Horn, Pierre L.
II. Pringle, Mary Beth, 1943–
PN56.5.P74145 1983   809'.933520692   83-18256
ISBN 0-8044-2702-X
ISBN 0-8044-6268-2 (pbk.)

To my wife:
Mary Beth Horn

To my husband:
Harvey A. Siegal

Contents

ACKNOWLEDGMENTS

The selection and preparation of the articles in this work have been shared equally by the editors.

We would like to express our thanks to the following people for their help in putting together this manuscript: Dean Eugene B. Cantelupe and members of the Liberal Arts Faculty Research Committee for their generous support; Professors Peter Bracher, Cecile Cary, David Garrison, John Park, all of whom suggested titles of books about prostitution and names of prostitutes from literature; and Mary Beth Horn and Leanne Smith for their excellent typing.

Introduction

PIERRE L. HORN AND MARY BETH PRINGLE

> So, if she has been called a woman of the town, a tart, a
> bawd, a wanton, a bawdy-basket, a bird-of-the-game,
> a bit of stuff, a buttered bun, a cockatrice, a cock-chafer,
> a cow, a crack, a cunt, a daughter of Eve, a gay girl, a
> gobble-prick, a high-flyer, a high-roller, a hussy, a hurry-
> whore, a jill, a jude, a judy, a jug, laced mutton, lift-
> skirts, light o'love, merry legs, minx, moll, moon-lighter,
> morsel, mount, mutton-broker, nestcock, night-bird,
> night-piece, night-walker, nymph of darkness, nymph of
> the pavement, petticoat, pick-up, piece, pillow-mate,
> pinch-prick, pole-climber, prancer, quail, quiet mouse,
> or even Queen—it is not surprising. A woman of lively
> parts is as likely to be slandered as she is to be praised.
>
> ERICA JONG
> *Fanny:*
> *Being the True History of the Adventures of*
> *Fanny Hackabout-Jones*

IT IS INTERESTING to note that in Erica Jong's long
list of synonyms for "prostitute" very few are also synonymous with a whole human being. Though the terms imply
the prostitute's working hours and conditions, denote parts of
her body, or compare her to various forms of animal life, rarely
do they grant her full personification. In fact these modes of

I

description, used satirically by Jong in the twentieth century, served to ensure that, in the eyes of the world, the prostitute of the eighteenth century remained an object.

Thus she has been seen in literature for centuries—as an object; a symbol, that revealed the patriarchal values and themes of the male writers who depicted her. For, with few exceptions, only men have dealt in fiction with prostitution. And their attitudes have been reinforced by male literary critics who largely have *not* been concerned with the social and political implications of the problem. Nor have these critics viewed holistically the psychology of prostitution; rather they have focused on the mind-set of the prostitute and ignored that of her customer.

Until very recently, the prostitute has been almost solely a "masculine" literary symbol. Why have not more women writers of fiction used prostitutes as main or secondary characters? What has kept female critics from grappling with the issues raised by prostitution? First, female fiction writers may have avoided incorporating the prostitute into their work because they had no contact with the demimonde. Lacking knowledge of the prostitute's environment and lifestyle, women writers have tended to keep their female characters in kitchens, drawing rooms, shops, schools, offices—places frequented by "respectable" women. Unlike male writers, females have tended to select images other than prostitution to symbolize individual weakness or social depravity. Second, not until heightened awareness brought women's roles and political problems to the fore in the 1970s did female critics begin to scrutinize more carefully the image of the prostitute in literature. And what they discovered was generally not to their liking.

Over and over again male writers have cast the prostitute in limited fictional roles, as a type rather than a real person. In fact, the prostitute almost always has been portrayed by men as one of the following archetypical figures:

The bitch-witch embodies wickedness and cruelty. She is a seductress who leads others to ruin or death, though authors seldom allow her to escape unscathed. Perhaps the best-known exemplar of this type is Nana in Emile Zola's novel of that name. With few redeeming qualities, she leaves misery and destruction in her wake, until at last she is punished by a hideous illness, becoming the incarnation of a nightmare. One wonders about the deep well of mysogyny from which such ghastly portrayals of the female surface. Because he fears and hates his own creation, the author who summons up the bitch-witch must destroy her before his work is finished.

The femme fatale resembles the bitch-witch, except that the author focuses on the prostitute's seductive qualities rather than her evil ones. A fine example of the femme fatale appears in Abbé Prévost's 1731 masterpiece, *Manon Lescaut.* The heroine is a demon with an angel's face. Coquettish, tender, but unthinking, she seduces men, bringing them momentary happiness, then suffering and sorrow. This archetype has a long history, traceable to Eve, who seduced the innocent Adam into the world of knowledge. Apparently as disturbing to men as the bitch-witch, the femme fatale triggers an often unconscious male fear of women's power and sexuality, both potential weapons of destruction.

The weak-but-wonderful prostitute is the whore-with-a-heart-of-gold. Despite her profession, she is often humane, loving, even innocent. Romanticism with its belief in the natural goodness of mankind was the ideal breeding ground for this type of literary heroine. She appeared as the title character in Victor Hugo's 1831 play, *Marion de Lorme,* and in England Charles Dickens embodies her in Nancy of *Oliver Twist* (1838). Twentieth-century examples of the tender, caring prostitute include Kitty Duval in William Saroyan's *The*

Time of Your Life (1939) and Adriana in Alberto Moravia's *The Woman of Rome* (1947).

The saved prostitute is essentially a virtuous woman who is redeemed from her profession. This conversion is usually brought about by a man who risks his reputation to save her. Thaïs in Anatole France's 1890 work by that name is a saved prostitute. So is Corrie in William Faulkner's *The Reivers* (1962), who is "cured" from the "sickness" of prostitution. It is interesting to note that there are relatively few saved prostitutes in literature; the more negative archetypes prevail.

The sinner-but-survivor is a product of the struggle to survive that leads some women into prostitution. The definition of "survival" is crucial here. For some literary heroines, such as Thackeray's Becky Sharp in *Vanity Fair* (1847), survival means living in luxury among the right social class. Carrie Meeber in Theodore Dreiser's *Sister Carrie* (1900) and Lily Bart in Edith Wharton's *House of Mirth* (1905) have similar requirements. For others, like Defoe's Moll Flanders, survival means only food on the table and a place to rest. Are Becky, Carrie, and Lily as much prostitutes as poor Moll? Again, a great deal depends upon definitions. None of the first three young women is shown accepting money for sexual favors: all three, however, use their bodies and cunning to obtain social standing and the wealth that goes with it.

The seduced-and-abandoned prostitute suffers a loss of virginity that leads her to a life in the streets. Stephen Crane's Maggie, for example, in *Maggie: A Girl of the Streets* becomes a prostitute after having been seduced and then cast out by her family. Dickens responded to this rather sentimental archetype by giving us two examples—Alice in *Dombey and Son* and Little Emily in *David Copperfield*.

The hapless harlot is an uncared-for victim of society. She is forced by misfortune and poverty into her degrading work. Unlike the sinner-but-survivor, this prostitute is never shown enjoying moments of comfort or success. Unlike the saved prostitute, she is not rescued from her situation, nor does she transform an unsatisfactory life into a tolerable one by her kindness or strength of character like the whore-with-a-heart-of-gold. Several realistic novels, especially twentieth-century works from Spain and Latin America, have portrayed this type of prostitute. Although this archetype is more realistic than some of the others, these novels focus more on the political and economic conditions that drive the women into prostitution than on the characterizations of the prostitutes themselves. Thus they become, for the reader and the critic, symbols rather than human beings.

The proud pro, although one of the less popular archetypes, does appear occasionally as the prostitute-turned-entrepreneur, the woman who builds a successful business around her trade. Perhaps the best-known exemplar is the title character in George Bernard Shaw's *Mrs. Warren's Profession* (1894). When Mrs. Warren's daughter insists that her mother give up her lucrative job as head of a chain of brothels, Mrs. Warren, proud of her success, refuses. Note that even here a prostitute's success and respectability are measured by the distance she puts between herself and the sexual aspects of her profession.

The cast-of-thousands are those prostitutes who have small walk-on parts in literature. They sometimes enter as nameless, faceless groups, and sometimes alone with a few moments to evoke the reader's disdain or sorrow. They function as foils for more important characters, typify the debased social setting in which they practice their trade, or represent the valueless life. They might embody the worst of an author's dreams or stand for the undelineated populations of brothels from Alexandria to Hong Kong. Finally, a male literary character's first visit to a faceless, nameless prostitute often symbolizes the onset of his manhood, an initiatory rite. In such cases, the prostitute becomes the disembodied symbol of a fallen world. Youthful purity meets impurity, and the innocent male youth finds himself immersed in putrid experience. These walk-ons are found in the works of male writers from William Shakespeare to J. D. Salinger, and they are the most depersonalized of all the archetypical prostitutes.

If male writers tend to stereotype the prostitute in fiction, how do female writers deal with her? The few women who have written about prostitutes tend to humanize them and treat them empathetically. Colette in her *Chéri* novels (1920 and 1929) describes in gentle, sensitive fashion the erotic relationship between an aging, motherly courtesan and her younger boyfriend. In *Fanny: Being the True History of the Adventures of Fanny Hackabout-Jones,* Erica Jong's title character is a picaresque heroine: strong, capable, gentle, and, finally, wise. As Amy Kaminsky's essay in this collection points out, Latin American writers Amalia Jamilis and Luisa Valenzuela emphasize the similarities, not the differences, between prostitutes and other women.

However, burden of placing meaning in a work of art does not lie entirely with its original creator. Critics (and other readers) play a central role in determining an image's (and a work's) meaning. Writing a story, novel, or play is a complex task that involves many personal and aesthetic choices. Identical issues come into play when a literary work is dealt with critically. Like the author who writes about a prostitute, the critic who comments on the character brings to the project her or his own experiences, prejudices, fears. In the act of interpretation, the critic consciously or unconsciously responds to the details and ideas expressed in the work through the overlay of these personal views. Clearly, this is a highly subjective process. Thus, readers who rely on criticism to explain literature should proceed with much caution. Criticism, giving us only one reader's view of a text, is by definition "imperfect."

In *The Image of the Prostitute in Modern Literature,* the editors have tried to be mindful of these creative and critical problems. Our goal has been not to explain the image of the prostitute as much as to raise questions about it. The reader, like the critics, will bring to the study of prostitution as literary image his or her own intellectual and emotional viewpoints. When deciding on a text's meaning, the reader will filter both the literary work and criticism about it through these personal lenses. Perhaps the best way to widen these lenses is to present the reader with a broad spectrum of critical interpretations.

In soliciting essays for this book, all but one of which were written expressly for this collection, we did not ask critics to use one specific approach, hoping to gather into these pages a wide range of recent criticism about prostitution in modern literature. We focused on criticism from the 1980s since we felt it would provide a balanced and perhaps more humanistic view of the subject, both because of its international focus and because the feminist movement of the seventies and eighties has encouraged critics as well as others to reexamine many of the traditional assumptions about women. Also spurred by the feminist movement, more criticism about the literary image of the prostitute is being written by women. The essays that follow then are written by both women and men, examine the image of the prostitute in the literatures of various areas of the world, and range from political studies of the prostitute's oppression to whimsical, romantic treatments of the mysteries of human relationships. We believe the reader will be enriched by these divergent views of the prostitute in modern literature.

The Prostitute as Scapegoat: Mildred Rogers in Somerset Maugham's *Of Human Bondage*

BONNIE HOOVER BRAENDLIN

> The best scapegoats, the only good scapegoats, really are the scapegoats who are not recognized as such.
>
> RENÉ GIRARD

SCARCELY ANY OTHER character in modern British fiction has been disparaged as unanimously as Mildred Rogers, the supercilious waitress turned prostitute in Somerset Maugham's early-twentieth-century *Bildungsroman, Of Human Bondage* (1915).[1] Critics of the novel have nearly all regarded Mildred solely from the author's viewpoint, perhaps because Maugham's naturalistic, detailed style so convincingly characterizes her as an immoral "slut" and castigates her as a representative of feminine evil, allowing her no redeeming virtue. Because Mildred is propelled into prostitution by her own snobbery, it is obvious that she is culpable and thus perhaps deserving of her fate, yet from other perspectives she appears not only as villainess but also as victim. In this novel

9

of male self-development, Mildred assumes the position of a scapegoat, compelled to expiate the sins of others, specifically those of the protagonist, Philip Carey, and more generally those of women who defy prescribed identities and demand proscribed freedoms. She is victimized in a symbolic way by the demands of the traditional male *Bildungsroman,* which sacrifices woman to man's development process and in a sociological sense by a rigid class hierarchy and propriety and by a paucity of opportunities for women to advance themselves or to find satisfying work. Her independent willfulness suggests her affinities with the New Woman, a turn-of-the-century phenomenon depicted in various guises by novelists of the period; her irrational destructiveness relates her to female demons and finally to all outsiders who avenge themselves against societal ostracism.

Of Human Bondage delineates a young man's struggle to realize his own identity, or in bourgeois terms, to achieve a successful integration into his society through the proper choice of vocation and wife; hence, the novel closely follows the basic pattern and philosophy of the conventional *Bildungsroman.* Maugham's novel continues the practice established by its predecessors in the *Bildungsroman* tradition—Goethe's *Wilhelm Meisters Lehrjahre* and Charles Dickens's *David Copperfield,* for example—of rewarding the mature adolescent with marriage to an idealized woman. Like Goethe's Natalie and Dickens's Agnes, Sally Athelny incarnates those female characteristics which men have usually considered ideal—unselfish love, unquestioning devotion, and uncritical maternal solicitude—against which all the other women in the novel, including Mildred, are measured and found wanting. On an archetypal level, Sally provides the means whereby Philip as the questing hero can reaffirm lost ties with the natural world.[2] Her affinity with nature becomes evident especially at the end of the novel as she emerges "a Saxon goddess"[3] in the hop fields of Kent. By virtue of her

sexual openness, Sally is a twentieth-century improvement on
the Victorian mother-goddess, a fitting reward for the young
modern who frees himself from outmoded religion and morality yet retains a sense of familial responsibility and societal
duty and of the necessity for harmony with the natural world,
which is all but eclipsed by industrialism and urbanization.

When Philip meets Sally, he has for some time been
hopelessly and helplessly enslaved by his irrational passion for
Mildred, whose commonness, vulgarity, and infidelity he de-
spises. The defects of several women in Philip's previous adolescent love affairs and friendships coalesce in Mildred's
repulsiveness, which is diametrically opposed to Sally's ideal
beauty. Mildred's tall, thin, drooping figure, flat chest, and
narrow hips characterize her as less than the established ideal
of feminine pulchritude, while her greenish, anemic skin tone
betrays her underlying unhealthiness. Her outer sickly physique masks no mitigating inner beauty or strength of character; her "common" and "vulgar" personality lacks any
redeeming "gentleness" or "softness" (pp. 258 – 86). In addition to being unfeminine, Mildred lacks "the maternal instinct" (p. 352), a grievous flaw for any woman to have in a
male *Bildungsroman,* in which the goal of individual and
societal stability depends on a perpetuation of values through
family solidarity and inheritance. The perfect wife not only
provides essential maternal solicitude for the struggling hero
but promises to give continuity to his newfound identity
through children, preferably sons.

Mildred is one of many characters sacrificed in this
Bildungsroman and in countless others to the development
process of the protagonist. Philip's inexplicable infatuation
with her constitutes one of the series of trials in his progress
toward maturity, illustrating the destructive power of un-
bridled emotion over reason, a major theme in Maugham's
novel.[4] Robert Lorin Calder points out that a destructive
female like Mildred appears in most English nineteenth- and

early-twentieth-century *Bildungsromane:* "It is usually part of a young man's apprenticeship that he becomes ensnared by a woman who is vulgar, insensitive and unintelligent. In most cases the hero finally frees himself and, although emotionally scarred, is more mature because of his experience."[5] Calder offers no explanation for the inclusion of such a character, but his remark implies that her presence, although appearing to hinder the protagonist's development, in some way furthers it. As seductress, Mildred incurs the blame for impeding Philip's progress, since her enslavement of him causes his initial failure in medical school and eventually contributes to his impoverishment. Yet she also promotes his progress by exemplifying the inevitable consequences of undesirable behavior and destructive emotions. Philip's devastating relationship with Mildred chastens his pride and strengthens his will and determination; most important, it demonstrates to him that love is not so much passion as affection and respect, two sensible emotions that he feels for Sally, although he does not "love" her.

As a symbol of enslaving emotional, irrational passion, Mildred represents that bane of male existence, the femme fatale, the unattainable temptress, the faithless lover, the social counterpart to the immortal fairy, *La Belle Dame sans Merci.* By refusing to submit to Philip's sexual advances because she feels neither sexual attraction nor love for him, Mildred illustrates Barbara Fass's definition of the femme fatale, "the unattainable temptress who keeps her admirer in a perpetual state of longing." Later, when Mildred turns to other men to satisfy her own desires, she fulfills another form of the archetype by becoming the "frequently faithless partner of a destructive love affair,"[6] although ironically the "affair" with Philip is devoid of love. Mildred appears to be damned if she does (with other men) and damned if she doesn't (with Philip). In *Of Human Bondage,* the specific social designation for the destructive female archetype is the prostitute, which Mildred becomes after Philip refuses to marry her because he is disgusted and disillusioned by her unfaithfulness. Prostitution brands Mildred a pariah, separated by an insurmountable gulf from respectable womanhood. Because she solicits men on the streets, taking them back to her dingy room, she inhabits the lowest rung of the demimonde social hierarchy, far removed from the courtesans in elegant brothels who catered to the Edwardian upper classes and thus enjoyed a measure of social respect and even envy.

Mildred's fall to the depths of depravity punishes her for sexual promiscuity, a conduct accepted as part of the normal course of events in a young man's adolescent development, in which his sexual exploits confirm his manhood. A comparison of Mildred's actions with Philip's indicates that her emotions, desires, and responses parallel his in reverse. The direction of Mildred's reaction to Philip during their relationship proves to be the inverse of the course of his interest in her. Her initial lack of response to Philip's advances leads Philip to conclude that she is impervious to passion, but gradually her sensuality emerges in her affairs with other men, at the same time that Philip's ardor cools in reaction to her "infidelity." She becomes as enslaved to passion as Philip is in the early stages of their acquaintanceship. Finally she turns her desires toward Philip, only to be rebuffed by his decision that their association be platonic. Mildred's reactions of bewilderment, humiliation, and anger, which are reported by the narrator just before her attack on Philip's room and mark one of the few lapses of the limited omniscient point of view, echo the "pique" and humiliation Philip demonstrates earlier. Calder provides a rationale for Mildred's destructiveness, attributing it to sexual frustration and loss of "mastery" over Philip once he no longer desires her,[7] two motives that also suggest her affinities with Philip. Mildred in fact personifies the very weakness of character that Philip himself displays and which hinder his development: Philip accuses her of being "on the make" (p. 285) as he himself is; she betrays him for other men, but he in turn betrays Norah Nesbitt when Mildred returns to him.

As is typical with secondary characters in a *Bildungsroman,* Mildred is allowed no self-development and no change of heart; but unlike other personages in *Of Human Bondage,* such as Norah, who is rescued by marriage, Mildred is denied redemption. The nature of Mildred's illness as a prostitute presages an early death for her. The fact that the severity of her punishment exceeds the enormity of her "crimes" and the fact that Philip escapes punishment for similar sins suggest that Mildred assumes the burden of Philip's guilt as well as her own. Her sins are his sins exaggerated, and her penalty is his release. As a scapegoat she is sacrificed so that Philip may be strengthened. As she deteriorates, he regenerates; as she slides down the social scale, he rises, moving from the poverty of his student days to the security of the medical profession.

As a scapegoat Mildred is both guilty and not guilty.[8] She represents the "fallen woman" who, although partly responsible for her own actions and choices, is also victimized by men in particular and society in general. Mildred's early conditioning, her petty bourgeois upbringing, has instilled in her a scorn for menial work like waitressing and a belief in the necessity of marriage for respectability and advancement on the social scale. The latter conviction conspires with her uncontrollable emotional desires to increase her vulnerability to men who seduce her by marriage offers or by affairs that end in deception and abandonment. Ironically, Mildred's vanity and desire for independence, in addition to her snobbish attitude—typical, Maugham says, of her class—cause her fall to a level of the social scale diametrically opposite that of the respected housewife she longs to become and pretends to be while living and traveling with Philip.

Maugham's unrelieved negative portrayal of Mildred in this novel differs from his more sympathetic treatment of prostitutes, such as Miss Sadie Thompson in "Rain" but resembles other characterizations of destructive women in his works.[9] One critic speculates that Mildred's despicable character results from Maugham's notorious misogyny occasioned by his disillusionment with women who could not measure up to his mother or assuage the pain occasioned by her death; others assume that Maugham's desire to expunge the memory of some agonizing love affair prompted his deleterious description of Mildred.[10] Both theories have merit, especially because *Of Human Bondage* is an autobiographical novel, detailing the pain suffered by a little boy who loses his beloved mother, as happened to Maugham.

Another possible explanation is suggested, however, by Mildred's affinities with the New Woman, the independent female who caused consternation in England from the 1890s into the twentieth century. While Mildred does not directly rival Philip for professional opportunities, she does threaten the accepted societal notion of male domination, which is essential to Philip's pride and easily bruised ego. At the beginning of their relationship, Philip cannot control Mildred although he is determined to bend her to his will. Later he feels betrayed when she follows her own passionate inclinations, and unjustly injured and insulted when she rebels against his mandate of a platonic liaison, destroying his property in revenge for his treatment of her.

When he attempts to rehabilitate her, to get her off the streets and prevent her from spreading venereal disease, she pushes him away with a final vituperative comment: "What do I care? Let them [the men she solicits] take their chance. Men haven't been so good to me that I need bother my head about them" (p. 543). Turning an independent woman into a diseased harpy suggests that Maugham's misogyny may have been furthered by a fear of the consequences inherent in woman's desire for self-determination and her refusal to acquiesce to maternal and subordinate roles; it may reveal some of the antagonism toward the New Woman expressed in other Edwardian literature, in novels such as H. G. Wells's *Tono-Bungay* and D. H. Lawrence's *Sons and Lovers*. Samuel Hynes attributes this hostility to the fear that women's desire for freedom presented a serious threat to family stability and hence to societal equilibrium, already shaken by disruptive factors resulting from increased industrialization.[11] While the young Edwardians desired more sexual freedom, even extending it to women as if to enhance them as sexual partners, they also regretted the loss of their Victorian fathers' ideal of a stable and sheltered home life safeguarded by a contented wife-mother. Mildred's characterization seems to incorporate this trepidation and desire for revenge on the wayward female; she may be Maugham's scapegoat for the New Woman, made to expiate her independent spirit.

Having demonstrated that Mildred becomes a scapegoat for the sins of others, we may extend the nature of her sacrifice by reference to her as a manifestation of the universal goddess, as the evil side of the Great Mother archetype.[12] If Sally is the "sinless" aspect of the deity in that she embraces her designated role as maternal helpmate, Mildred represents the misguided goddess who resists. In a response to Claude Lévi-Strauss's observations on myth, René Girard defines one basic mythic structure as the ritual elimination of an erring deity, the scapegoating of a divine being who has acted in a manner threatening to the community. If a society's crisis situation is severe enough and the causes vague, an individual deity or a human incarnation may be accused and made a scapegoat even though not guilty of any real crime or causative action. From the perspective of the threatened community, the apparent malefactor or a helpless substitute is always guilty; and the punishment, usually ostracism or death, is always justified.[13] In *Of Human Bondage*, Mildred is made a scapegoat to save Philip from his personal crisis, but in a larger sense, she is sacrificed for the good of a society in crisis. Although, as

Calder says, Maugham's novel in many ways "attempts to grapple with man's new freedom in the twentieth century,"[14] it reaffirms traditional answers to modern dilemmas, particularly those involving threatened values such as the stable home as a bulwark against change. The marriage of Sally and Philip at the end of the novel is intended to restore a threatened societal ideal; it is Maugham's answer to his culture's crisis, and it necessitates the death of Mildred, the erring goddess.

Widening the circle of those who benefit from the ostracism and death of a scapegoat enables us to see Mildred as an example of the "outsider," defined by Vivian Gornick as "one in whom experience lives in a metaphorical sense, one whose life and meaning is a surrogate for the pain and fear of existence, one onto whom is projected the self-hatred that dogs the life of the race." Like Sue Bridehead in Thomas Hardy's *Jude the Obscure*, Mildred incarnates "the quintessential female" whose "behavior is emotional, impetuous, illogical, uncontrollable," all characteristics that help explain Mildred's supposedly inexplicable destructiveness. When she annihilates Philip's possessions, presumably in a streak of mad fury, Mildred demonstrates "the infantilism of reduction" typical of all outsiders who are denied the advantages of civilized living appropriated by the inside elite. Finally, as the fatally diseased prostitute, she becomes the scapegoat, described by Gornick as one whose "life is offered up, as every outsider's life is offered up, as a sacrifice to the forces of annihilation that surround our sense of existence, in the hope that in reducing the strength of the outsider—in declaring her the bearer of all the insufficiency and contradiction of the race—the wildness, grief, and terror of loss that is in us will be grafted onto her, and the strength of those remaining within the circle will be increased."[15] Mildred, the diseased prostitute, the treacherous goddess, the independent woman, dies for us all.

Critics of Maugham's novel maintain that reader sympathy for Philip continues even when he appears ridiculous by wishing that he could stab Mildred in the carotid artery with his muffin knife or callous by longing for his uncle's death so that he can get his inheritance. Maugham's vituperative treatment of Mildred as unredeemed feminine evil supposedly excludes any similar compassion for her, yet it may in fact engender sympathetic understanding. Even as a spiteful fallen woman, Mildred exhibits a measure of courage and independence by scorning the option of serving a man who neither loves nor respects her. Sympathy for Mildred and her plight comes more easily perhaps to readers whose consciousness has been raised by the women's movement and feminist criticism. But Maugham's naturalistic technique, which revels in sordid detail in order to expose the evils of society (as in the slum where Philip practices medicine) and to revive a threatened societal ideal, may in Mildred's case also contribute to a sympathetic reading of her character and function by affording a view of her as a representation of a social reality, the fallen woman and unwed mother, a victim as well as a villainess, a person as well as a symbol.

Of Human Bondage is undeniably remarkable for its particular vindictiveness toward the threatening female, which transforms her into a prostitute who, as scapegoat, is sacrificed for all who remain within the circle of respectability and rationality. Even this vindictiveness, though, may backfire by loading the dice against Mildred and thus increasing reader sympathy for her. Because Maugham advances the time-honored theme of ironic comedy that the scapegoat must be ritualistically expunged from society, his treatment of Mildred may illustrate Northrop Frye's contention that "insisting on the theme of social revenge on an individual, however great a rascal he [or she] may be, tends to make him [or her] look less involved in guilt and the society more so."[16]

French Feminist Theater and the Subject of Prostitution, 1870–1914

AMY MILLSTONE

REFERENCES TO SEXUALITY, particularly female sexuality, dominate the French theater of the period 1870–1914. The critic Maurice Descotes points to the scandalous success of Dumas *fils*'s *La Dame aux camélias* (1852) as the turning point in the dramatic treatment of this theme because according to him, it was the first play to describe in great detail the life of a *demi-mondaine*.[1] Interest in the play was aroused when it was censored by the Minister of the Interior, and subsequent to the lift of this ban, women of the bourgeoisie flocked to the theater for this dramatic first because, as Dumas's contemporary, the critic Jules Janin stated, "Honest women want to know how other women live and die."[2] As a result of the triumph of *La Dame aux camélias*, the theme of sexuality began to dominate the theater, not only for the generation which claimed Dumas *fils* as its principal dramatist (1850–1870) but for the following one as well. Moreover, a great majority of plays which dealt essentially with sexuality usually limited their treatment to one of several variations of illicit sexuality: the "fallen" girl or woman, the love triangle, the "kept" woman, or the prostitute.

19

In his treatment of the theme of prostitution, Dumas *fils* merely brought to the stage an attitude that had been present in French literature since the Enlightenment. As Mario Praz has shown, "This theme of the prostitute regenerated by love ... was destined, with the Romantics, to become one of the chief points of their cult of tainted beauty."[3] However, the Romantics largely channeled their efforts in this vein into poetry and the novel. Dramatists of the Romantic period such as Mérimée (*Le Carrosse du Saint-Sacrement,* 1852) and Hugo (*Marion de Lorme,* 1831) occasionally treated the theme of prostitution, but in setting the action of their plays in other countries and time periods, they could at once indulge a Romantic predilection for theme as well as for exotic climates and the lure of the past, thus escaping the stigma of portraying "current events," as did Dumas *fils.* With Dumas, the "whore with the heart of gold" was inextricably linked to current society and became a sacrosanct convention for theater from his time forth. At the same time, however, Dumas's depiction of the expiation of sin ultimately reassured rather than attacked conventional morality, and hence the theatergoing public could accept the presentation of immorality on the stage.

Feminists of the post-Dumas period were highly critical of the limited and one-sided representation of women on the stage. In an 1866 public lecture entitled "La Femme dans le théâtre," Maria Deraismes complained that her contemporaries "prefer to limit themselves, in accordance with the old traditions, to the spectacle of woman created for man, subordinate to him, subject to his law, expecting everything from his whims; consequently, taking pains to please him, serve him, devote herself to him."[4] Furthermore, she cautioned that such a distorted image of women in the theater had dangerous implications in real life: "We recognize that, in this domain [the theater], man composes woman according to prejudices and his passions, and that woman, in turn, models herself upon this fantastic creation."[5] Even after the turn of the century, some feminists felt that significant progress had not been made in the theater: "Underneath her elegant finery, she [the woman] is merely a plaything, plaything of man, plaything of events, and sometimes a recalcitrant, maleficent plaything, but always a plaything, due to her ignorance."[6]

In an attempt to combat the pernicious effects of limited portrayals of women in the theater, feminist playwrights created new dramatic situations for women. At the same time, they expanded their definition of prostitution to include the hallowed institution of marriage. By so doing, they merely brought to the stage a parallel which had been established in nondramatic literature of the Romantic period. As early as the 1830s and 1840s, utopian socialists such as Fourier, Saint-Simon, and Flora Tristan had compared the marriage of convenience to prostitution on the grounds that both institutions denied the woman free expression of emotional and sexual love. George Sand was one of the leading exponents of this point of view in many of her novels. Marx, and particularly Engels, continued and expanded this critique by attacking the economic foundations of both institutions. French feminists, however, were unaware of Engels's theories until the 1890s[7] and were even hostile to socialism because in France, the working-class movement was led by the great antifeminist Proudhon. Paradoxically, it was the desire to discredit Proudhon's dictum ("housewife or courtesan") that led French feminists — and hence feminist dramatists — to formulate parallels between marriage and prostitution, such as those which Engels codified in his epic work *Origins of the Family, Private Property and the State.*[8]

Three overlapping themes were particularly exploited by feminist dramatists to establish the parallel between marriage and prostitution. Although the following points of discussion may be said to pertain to the aristocracy as well as the bourgeoisie and to a lesser extent the middle classes, the analysis derives from a bourgeois concept of marriage and was applied by feminist dramatists almost exclusively to women of the bourgeoisie.

First and foremost was a critique of the marriage of convenience as a form of prostitution. In the short one-act play *Se marier* (1906), Jeanne Marni criticizes—through two women's comments about a third—women of the bourgeoisie who prefer to marry anyone with money rather than try to assure their economic survival through independent struggle. The explanation for such voluntary prostitution, according to Madame Marni, is the socialization of bourgeois women to accepted sex-role and behavioral norms. Indeed, as Françoise d'Eaubonne has shown, women were trained to view marriage as the only career to which an "honest" woman could aspire: "The education of a well-heeled young woman tends to turn her into a luxurious parasite; she is duped, she is amused with frills, playthings and madrigals; she is permitted the arts of refinement, as are the geisha or the hetaera, but she is denied serious study and culture . . . those few signs which would open the mind."[9] Hence, though Lucy Joquouy—the woman criticized in the play—was counseled by some to buy an umbrella shop and live by her own toil, she preferred to marry anyone (rich) rather than work.

Just as women sought to marry in order to gain social status as well as financial security, so did men seek in marriage a respite from the economic and physical strains wrought by years of dissolute behavior. In order to establish the link between the bourgeois marriage of convenience and prostitution clearly for both men and women, feminist dramatists focused on the manner in which each sex was enticed into matrimony by the other.

Men generally were depicted as selling themselves through their wealth or power. In *Se marier* Lucy Joquouy's husband is depicted not as a person to whom Lucy is married but rather as "the monster: six million francs and a historic château."[10] In most feminist plays of the period 1870–1914, husbands are depicted in equally inhuman ways. However, unlike Madame Marni, who deplored the stereotyping of men as much as that of women, the majority of playwrights portrayed men as monsters in an attempt to create a climate of sympathy for the women victimized by such men. Thus, the psychological motivation of women who revolt against abusive male authority appears not only understandable but imperative as well.

For women, the dowry functioned as an unhealthy lure for husbands, just as for men, titles or property served to attract women. Perhaps the most dramatic representation of this theme is the use of the costume as a means of seduction, as important to the young woman trying to attract a husband as to the prostitute seeking a client. Moreover, the use of costume as a means of entrapment of husbands underscored the fact that women ultimately had only their physical selves to sell, being deprived of independent wealth and totally devoid of real power. In each case, the costume chosen is in strict accordance with the social roles the women are to play. Ironically, in their use of costume to entice men, bourgeois women and prostitutes reverse roles.

In *Les Trois Filles de M. Dupont* (1897), Eugène Brieux dramatizes the courtship and subsequent marriage of Julie, a well-bred bourgeois woman. As soon as she has accepted a marriage proposal, Julie's parents urge her to change clothing before the arrival of her fiancé and his parents. When her mother explicitly tells her to don her finest ball gown, Julie is prompted to ask: "Is it my dress that he will marry?"[11] Her question is certainly understandable. Because her flirtation is to be rewarded with marriage, and because it is assumed that she is a virgin, Julie is permitted to be openly provocative, to show her shoulders and bust. Not only does her gown put her at an advantage but just as importantly, a ball gown is elegant and provides ample proof of the social standing of the parents.

The prostitute, on the other hand, must play on the

sexual fantasies of her clients. As Sheila Rowbotham has pointed out, "Bourgeois man located in the prostitute, who was often seen as synonymous with the lower-class woman, all the sensuality denied to his own women. . . . "[12] Consequently, prostitutes often disguised themselves as working-class women. In his shocking play *Les Avariés* (1901), Brieux depicts a prostitute who describes the details of her profession. She dresses in special clothes that will make her look like a working woman and hurries down the street to create the illusion that she is indeed an honest woman. Periodically, she stops to gaze into a store window, and it is then that she is solicited. A respectable appearance is crucial for the prostitute because the client who is willing to pay for the fantasy of seducing a working-class woman would not risk a sexual encounter if the woman betrayed signs of being what she is, that is, a potential transmitter of venereal disease.[13]

A second parallel between the prostitute and the married bourgeois woman is established through women's analysis of sexuality as a power struggle. During the nineteenth century, two contradictory notions of the role of sexuality within marriage coexisted. On the one hand, the husband was defined as the sole teacher and beneficiary of his wife's sexuality, and sex was predicated on *his* sole desire; on the other hand, sexuality was viewed as a legitimate weapon to be used by women over their husbands, either to obtain presents or favors or to ward off rivals. In perhaps the only monolog of its kind in the period, the high-spirited heroine of *Autour du mariage* (1883) by Gyp muses about her sexual initiation the night before and laments her own ignorance: "I think I will get whatever I want from him by appealing to his . . . sentiments. . . . I would hold him more solidly if I knew a lot of things that I am ignorant of . . . the strings of the profession, in short. . . . "[14] Paulette envies the prostitute her greater experience with the tricks of the trade. Similarly, the heroines of a Paul Hervieu drama, *L'Enigme* (1901), are advised by a friend to regain their husbands' trust in the bedroom: "Cease to overwhelm your husbands with protestations. Run and join them in your bedrooms. There is your place, there is your empire. . . . "15

Bourgeois women who thus feel inferior to prostitutes because of the latter's greater experience and apparent freedom of choice of clients usually are disillusioned by the professionals whom they encounter in feminist plots. In *Les Trois Filles de M. Dupont*, Julie wants to leave her husband. She is urged to stay with him by her eldest sister, Angèle, who became a prostitute after she was abandoned by the man who seduced her. According to Angèle, there is in fact little difference between her own lot and her sister's, but the difference that does exist—many clients as opposed to one, the husband—is sufficient to make her envy her sister's plight.16 As a married woman, Julie is at least entitled to the social respect and minimal legal protection that are totally denied to the prostitute.

The only advantage that prostitutes seem to hold over their married counterparts is lucidity about their position. From the very start, the prostitute realizes that hers is a struggle for economic survival and that love or any other form of sentiment is totally absent from her work. In *Les Hannetons* (1906), another Brieux drama, Charlotte has a brutally frank discussion with her lover in which she tells him that she has never loved him:

PIERRE: Why did you yield to me then?
CHARLOTTE: You've already asked me that. . . . You want me to say that I was seduced by your handsome physique or by your position? No, my friend. If you got me, it's because when I met you . . . it was the off-season.
PIERRE: During your unemployment you needed a companion?
CHARLOTTE: Not even. A purse.
PIERRE: For your ribbons?
CHARLOTTE: For my bread.17

The last theme that assimilates marriage to prostitution is that of sexuality as a vehicle of revenge against a man or men. For the bourgeois woman, premarital or extramarital sex is presented in feminist drama as the most effective way to inflict punishment on the father or husband in that the man's good name and honor are stained. Ironically, it is a courtesan who most clearly states the hypocrisy of bourgeois honor codes. In *Les Hannetons,* Pierre accuses Charlotte of infidelity. She tells him to forget her lapse:

> PIERRE: I can't: the whole house knows it too.
> CHARLOTTE: You don't mind being deceived: you just don't want to seem ridiculous.[18]

The details in adultery plays vary, but three clear patterns emerge. In some, the husband blames himself for his wife's infidelity and consequently forgives her; in others, adultery is the reason invoked for a divorce, in the course of which the woman is completely dehumanized; and in a few plays, the wife pays for her transgression with her life. All three solutions "conform" to reality, particularly since female adultery was much more easily sustained and more heavily punishable by law, even after the reestablishment of divorce in 1884.

The prostitute, on the other hand, did not stain a man's reputation but could potentially punish him in his person through the transmission of venereal disease. Such an option, far from revolutionary, must be interpreted as the only method of reprisal available to women who were bound by their profession to the very instruments of their oppression: men. At the end of *Les Avariés,* a prostitute confesses to the doctor—the dramatist's spokesperson—that she blamed men for her lowly life and wanted to punish them:

> These bastards give you a horrible disease and it's me they throw in prison. . . . It's a little too much. . . . Yes, but there was a fight. . . . Before they put me in Saint-Lazare, the very day that I knew I was caught, I was on my way

home, furious naturally . . . boulevard Saint-Denis, you
know who I run into? . . . My old boss. . . . I say to
myself: you, my friend, now's the time to make you pay
what you owe me . . . with interest. . . . I play up to
him. . . . Oh, it didn't take long. . . . And when I left him,
I don't know what rage possessed me . . . I took all those
that wanted . . . for what they offered . . . for nothing if
they offered nothing . . . and the youngest and hand-
somest. . . . I was only giving back what they'd given
me. . . . [19]

The analogy that bourgeois marriage equals prostitution,
as established in plays dealing with the sexual exploitation of
women, illustrates the dialectical function of feminist drama
in that women of various social classes are portrayed as victims of the same oppressive code. In so doing, feminist dramatists give expression to a notion of a panfeminism which
transcends class barriers. Statistically, however, few feminist
plays of the period 1870–1914 deal with prostitution per se,
concentrating instead on its bourgeois expression. Why this
reticence to fully investigate the real world? Part of the answer
lies in the authors themselves. The men and women who
wrote for the stage were themselves intellectuals of bourgeois
origin, and hence they often lacked a real understanding of
other women's lives. At the same time, the socioeconomic
makeup of the audience was essentially bourgeois and aristocratic. Women of these classes were primarily interested in
seeing *their* lives unfold on stage (with some exception), and
furthermore, they were generally sheltered from the problems
of other classes. Hence, bourgeois women frequently were
shown in interaction with women of other classes (servants,
for example), or their situation was compared with that of
other women (prostitutes) in an attempt to make the public
realize that women of all classes often share the same
problems.

Zola's View of Prostitution in *Nana*

JILL WARREN

Emile Zola's *Nana* (1880) is in part a study of a bourgeois author's views of prostitution and of the prostitute's aspirations to rise to a bourgeois existence. Nana exemplifies almost all the possible roles of the prostitute: the elegant courtesan, the common streetwalker, the rouée of very young men, the latent lesbian, and the lover prostituting herself for her man. Indeed, the novel contains many levels of prostitution. Zola, in attempting to present both the socioeconomic and the biological aspects of female sexuality through the metaphor of prostitution, produces a fascinating but rather chaotic and crowded novel that is artistically flawed because it tries to do too much. However, as a record of male mistrust of female sexuality, it is a document worthy of study. Zola records some widely held misapprehensions and is a barometer of attitudes toward women at the time, in contrast to a writer such as Henrik Ibsen, whose Nora in *A Doll's House* (1870) predicts what many women would become.

That Zola's view of female sexuality is representative of his age can be demonstrated by reference to his methods of composition. Zola's art was one of observation, recording, and synthesis. Characteristically, he researched each novel thoroughly and observed several examples of his subject before he began to write. When he conceived the idea of studying the decadence of the Second Empire leading to its collapse in 1870 through the examination of a courtesan, he began going to the theater and making the acquaintance of several real-life courtesans, such as Blanche d'Antigny, Hortense Schneider, and Cora Pearl.[1] Furthermore, his theory of naturalism, that human behavior is determined by scientific laws and biological drives which can be observed and recorded, is well known. Taking great pains to give the impression of scientific detachment and objectivity to his Rougon-Macquart cycle, Zola presents a physical or hereditary explanation for every action or characteristic. For example, Nana's amoral attitude toward sex can be traced to her childhood, depicted in *L'Assommoir* (1887), when she not only was given no moral instruction but actually witnessed her mother Gervaise and her stepfather Coupeau in the sex act. The most degraded of her lovers, Comte Muffat, can trace his insatiable appetite for sex to a hereditary legacy from his father, the Marquis de Chouard, and to a lifetime of sexual repression. Zola is a keen observer of human behavior, and his pen can record vividly what his eye sees. He is, as his friend Paul Brulet described him,

> the psychologist of the multitudes. . . . His characters are not at all exceptional human beings, they are general types, incarnating collectivities, the miseries, the state of mind and soul of a whole category of individuals, of a whole social class. It is there that Zola's work, rough as a breath, the smell exhaled from the crowds, is a formidable democratic epic.[2]

His writing is, therefore, an excellent indicator of the prevailing attitude of his times.

The logical fallacy in the naturalistic theory that scientific laws of human behavior can become the basis of a literary method often has been articulated by critics, such as J. G. Patterson, who stated that

> The "experiments" by the novelist cannot be made on subjects apart from himself but are made by him, and in him; so that they prove more regarding his own temperament than about what he professes to regard as the inevitable actions of his characters. The conclusion drawn by a writer from such actions must always be open to the retort that he invented the whole himself. . . . [3]

Therefore, in examining the prostitute in *Nana*, Zola, while attempting scientific detachment, has unconsciously recorded his own bourgeois attitudes. Furthermore, those attitudes were formed partly by his participation in the *Zeitgeist* as a child growing up in Second Empire France and partly by his meticulous researches, which made him a representative composite of his age. When, in Nana's immense attractiveness, he shows an elemental fear of the power of female sexuality; when, in Nana's ruin of Steiner, Vandeuvres, and Muffat, he shows that survival of the fittest means that the female will use her sexual power to achieve a social and economic advance at the expense of the weaker males; when, in Nana's acceptance of abuse by Fontan, he shows that the female will be aroused sexually only by a stronger, more brutal male; and when, in Sabine Muffat's affair with Fauchery, he shows that a respectable married woman's awakening to sexual passion will degrade her, Zola records the tangled attitudes toward female sexuality held during his time.

Perhaps some readers are surprised at the label of *"bourgeois"* for Zola, the man who wrote frankly of many subjects never before treated in serious literature and who was condemned in his own time as a pornographer. An anecdote recorded by Leon Edel in his biography of Henry James reveals James's discovery that Zola's use of "dirty" subjects was completely innocent. James had thought of *Nana* as a "combination of the cesspool and the house of prostitution" and had disliked Zola's subject matter until he heard him one day at Flaubert's describe how he was compiling for himself a dictionary of coarse language to write *L'Assommoir.* James had been struck with "the tone in which he made the announcement—without bravado and without apology, as an interesting idea that had come to him and that he was working, really, to arrive at character and particular truth, with all his conscience." James goes on to say that Zola "had marched from subject to subject and had 'got up' each in turn."[4] Far from being an immoral debaucher recording his own experience, Zola was a morally earnest, inexperienced, judgmental bourgeois who was as shocked at what his researches uncovered as his readers were.

Zola's judgment of Nana's sexuality can be seen in his description of her in his *ébauche,* or preliminary outline, for the novel:

> The philosophical subject is as follows: a whole society hurling itself at the cunt. A pack of hounds after the bitch who is not even in heat and makes fun of the hounds following her. The poem of male desires, the great lever which moves the world. There is nothing apart from the cunt and religion.[5]

The word "cunt" here is meant as a scientific, anatomical term intended to strip away romantic illusions about love being a significant part of sexual attraction. Even if the less vulgar word "vagina" were substituted by the translator, these notes would still reveal a fundamental fear and hatred of the power of female sexual attractiveness. The analogy of people to hounds and bitch in the next sentence is intended to liken humanity to the animal kingdom and thus to eliminate the need to consider the heart or the conscience as the base of human attraction, an analogy in keeping with the naturalist's attempt at social Darwinism. However, the misogynistic implications of using the word "cunt" as a synecdoche for the woman herself cannot be avoided.

Here Zola reveals the feeling that those who succumb to this power are fools courting their own ruin. Zola does not respond to female sexuality as did D. H. Lawrence, his near contemporary, who also feared the evil, mysterious power he saw in the female principle but who also said that there is a greater, more positive, rejuvenating power in the penis. Nor does Zola grant that Nana's powerful sexuality might be regarded as the power of fecundity, that of the voluptuous, nurturing earth mother. Indeed, her only offspring, Louiset, is an inferior specimen, and though she becomes pregnant (and miscarries) once more in the novel, she does not conceive nearly as often as one might expect, given the frequency of opportunity. Zola, however, does not consider the question of who is responsible for this barrenness, Nana herself or the impotent men with whom she couples or both. Rather, Zola's response seems to be one of fear and fascination, attraction to and repulsion from the female principle. Thus, in *Nana*, female sexuality in the form of prostitution becomes a symbol for unrestrained libido, for horror at the great power that female attraction exerts over men, and for the kind of evil that rotted Nana and the Second Empire from the inside out. This feeling that there is something horribly evil at the core of the human psyche, something that if not kept in check will gallop out of hand, has been shared by many other writers, notably another of Zola's contemporaries, Joseph Conrad, in *Heart of Darkness* (1902), but few others besides Zola have equated this horror so much with sex.

By intending to write the poem of male desires, Zola again shows his antifeminine bias. Nana is not a real woman at all but rather an antifeminist projection of a repressed and relatively inexperienced man's worst fears of woman. She is also a fantasy of the ideal sexual object, equipped as she is with a luscious body capable of incredible sexual endurance and always available if one has the price. Zola never attempts to explore female desires, nor does he seem inclined to imagine that they exist. Nana takes lovers not for her own pleasure but to pay her bills and break up the monotony of her life. She is fond of some, maternal toward others, and contemptuous of a few, but she herself never seems to be fulfilled by her sexual encounters. As Zola portrays her, she enjoys fondling her own body more than she enjoys masculine embraces, prefers Fontan's slaps to anyone else's kisses, and shares more intimacy with her sister prostitute Satin than with any of the men. There is never any hint that Nana's ennui about sex might be due to her male lovers' selfishness and lack of concern with her emotional needs, as there might be if Ibsen were writing the story. The commodity of sexuality is bought dearly, a simple supply and demand arrangement, and Zola cannot seem to perceive that Nana could want or get anything more than economic fulfillment.

In his *ébauche* Zola goes on to describe Nana's character as

> good-natured above all else. . . . Ends up regarding man as a material to exploit, becoming a force of Nature, a ferment of destruction, but without meaning to, simply by means of her sex and her strong female odor, destroying everything she approaches, and turning society sour just as women having a period turn milk sour. The cunt in all its power; the cunt on an altar, with all the men offering up sacrifices to it. The book will be the poem of the cunt, and the moral will lie in the cunt turning everything sour. . . . Nana eats up gold, swallows up every sort of wealth; the most extravagant tastes, the most frightful waste. Everything she devours; she eats up what people are earning in industry, on the stock exchange, in high positions, in everything that pays. And she leaves nothing but ashes. In short, a real whore (pp. 12 – 13).

This plan shows how closely Zola stuck to his first conception of the novel. If one still doubts that Zola failed in his attempts to employ the scientific method in his fiction, surely the old wives' tale about menstruating women and milk provides the final proof.

When Zola terms Nana a "real whore," he is not singling her out as unusual or different from other women, even respectable married women. Zola seems to feel that if he scratches a lady, he will find a whore (or a procuress), and that if he scratches a gentleman, he will find a sexual beast. The aristocratic counterpart to Nana is Countess Sabine Muffat, who, repressed like her husband, nonetheless falls into a torrid affair with the journalist Fauchery. With a practiced eye Fauchery notes the sleeping sexuality in Sabine at their first meeting and even speculates on a superficial similarity to Nana. "A mole, which he noticed on the Countess's left cheek, close to her mouth, suddenly attracted his attention. The curious thing was that Nana had precisely the same mole" (p. 81). Fauchery lays siege to the countess's virtue, and she allows herself to be seduced. After that, she begins to spend money as extravagantly as Nana and to lie to the count to conceal her clandestine rendezvous, as does Nana. Later, even the unperceptive Muffat realizes that respectability is mostly a matter of outward appearances: "A naked Nana evoked a naked Sabine. At this vision, which brought them together in a shameless relationship, under the influence of the same desire, he [Muffat] stumbled into the roadway, and a cab nearly ran over him" (pp. 230–31). Further evidence that Zola regarded all women as being essentially the same as Nana in character if not in physical endowments is revealed by the fact that all men go to an evening salon at Sabine's on a Tuesday and then to a midnight supper at Nana's on Wednesday. Although the assemblage of respectable women at the former is exchanged for courtesans at the latter, the evening features the same conversation about Bismarck, the same bourgeois attitudes, and the same triviality, with the men saying the same things on each occasion.

In *Nana,* prostitution becomes a metaphor for the decadent state of the nation during the Second Empire, and as such, it reveals the very fiber of life as felt by Zola. That the

Second Empire is hopelessly decayed is revealed in *Nana*'s very first chapter, in which we see the decline of culture at the theater, where the play *The Blond Venus*, the vehicle for Nana's acting debut, is a farcical look at Olympus in terms that describe Zola's contemporary society. The play involves seductions, cuckoldry, deception, and empty marriages: all the elements Zola will go on to dissect in the novel. Zola's own description makes his point eloquently: "This carnival of the gods, this dragging of Olympus in the mud, this mockery of a whole religion, a whole world of poetry, struck the audience as rich entertainment" (p. 39). Thus, the *Théâtre des Variétés*, as a commercial enterprise, gives the people what they want. In the audience or backstage is every character who will be seduced by Nana or fall under her influence, all thunderstruck by her talentless but powerful, nearly naked form on stage. Even that scion of the status quo, the theater critic, shows his titillation by laughing at the play before he hypocritically writes a scathing and shocked review of it. As Venus, Nana and her sexuality hypnotize the audience, despite her inability to act or sing:

> And Nana, in front of this fascinated audience, these fifteen hundred human beings crowded together and overwhelmed by the nervous exhaustion which comes towards the end of a performance, remained victorious by virtue of her marble flesh, and that sex of hers which was powerful enough to destroy this whole assembly and remain unaffected in return (p. 47).

Indeed, her sexual presence is so eloquent that Bordenave, the crafty theater manager, perceives speech to be superfluous and later has her appear in a play speaking no lines at all. In this later play, as in *The Blond Venus*, she is a hit; "she took the audience's breath away simply by showing herself" (p. 459).

The novel comes full circle, back to the image of Venus, but this time "Venus was decomposing. It was as if the poison she had picked up in the gutters, from the carcasses left there by the roadside, that ferment with which she had poisoned a whole people, had now risen to her face and rotted it" (p. 470). Nana, whose birth had corresponded to the rise of the Second Empire, dies in 1870, as the Second Empire dies, with crowds screaming "À Berlin" outside her deathbed window. She dies, disgustingly, of smallpox, with the disease sparing her no possible disfigurement. With this ending, Zola makes a powerful statement about the parallels betwen Nana's rottenness and the decay of her society, but the ending is somewhat contradictory.

Smallpox may be taken as a euphemism for venereal disease and so may suggest the genitals as the source of rottenness that surfaces at Nana's death. Also, Nana, unlike Flaubert's Emma Bovary, has gone through life largely unpunished for her sexual liberties, but like Oscar Wilde's Dorian Gray, she has her debaucheries recorded at last in the countenance of her death mask. Thus, smallpox in one sense suggests the ghastly culmination of Nana's private and public careers. However, the disease was contracted in one of the few noble, motherly actions Nana makes: the nursing of her child Louiset through a case of smallpox. Also, Nana's disease occasions the only affection her sister courtesans, especially archrival Rose Mignon, ever show for her, as though Nana's hideous death clarified for the courtesans their own condition and helped them see connections one to the other. It is Rose who devotedly nurses Nana and who says, "You know it's a great blow to me. . . . We were never nice to each other in the old days. And yet this has driven me out of my senses. . . . I've got all sorts of strange ideas, wanting to die myself, and feeling the end of the world coming" (p. 469). Here, in an apocalyptic view, even Rose instinctively equates Nana's end with the end of the Second Empire and with a foreshadowing of her own death. Just as in the first chapter, all the characters closely associated with Nana are assembled—the courtesans, the merchants of sex—in the room with her, and the men, the consumers, afraid to look on the decayed flesh they had once desired, are assembled on the street below her window.

Among those people who assemble at the novel's beginning to witness Nana's debut and reassemble throughout it in salons, at suppers, races, and finally at Nana's demise, there are specific examples of specific types of decadence, all drawn to the power of sex as exemplified in Nana. The wealthy banker Steiner, exemplar of the business world, eventually embezzles funds from an investment venture for her. Representing the aristocracy, Count Vandeuvres, apparently bent on ruining his family's ancient holdings, sacrifices his last lands to her. Representing the new generation, the young Hugon brothers, Georges and Philippe, commit suicide and go to jail, respectively, for desire of her. Even princes and heads of state frankly pay homage to Nana's sexuality. But the man most profoundly affected is the religious fanatic Comte Muffat, whose religious zeal seems to be a form of sublimated sexuality.[6] His utter abandonment of self, reputation, and fortune to Nana suggests that Zola anticipated some of Freud's theories about repression and guilt. Muffat is marked by

> the sort of passion peculiar to a man who has had no youth. . . . Woman dominated him [Muffat] with the jealous tyranny of a God of wrath, terrifying him but granting him moments of joy as keen as spasms, in return for hours of hideous torments, visions of hell and eternal tortures. . . . He would submit shudderingly to the omnipotence of sex, just as he would swoon before the mysterious power of heaven (pp. 427, 440).

To Zola, Muffat's capacity for passionate devotion to the church shows him capable of a fanatical devotion to sin as well. Furthermore, the church's power is pale compared with the power of sex. Muffat cannot save himself by an appeal to heaven.

Muffat also demonstrates the complete ruin of the aristocracy by Nana concomitant with her own desire for economic advance. Muffat is not in the least attractive to Nana, and she uses him purely for her own financial advancement. Although elsewhere in the Rougon-Macquart cycle, Zola admits into his fiction the Marxist notion that the proletariat will naturally attempt to rise up to the level of the bourgeoisie (as in *Germinal* [1885]), he does not in Nana's case regard such a struggle as glorious. He regards Nana's fight for such a rise with true loathing because of its ruthlessness and its roots in sex. Recognizing that her only access to power and wealth is through her sexuality, Zola shows her using her body in an orgy of self-indulgence in material things in an attempt to put an end to her ennui, caused by the succession of lifeless men who attempt to reinvigorate themselves through contact with her vitality. Had Zola been less a judgmental bourgeois steeped in middle-class morality, he might have seen Nana as a pitiful victim whose sexuality made her a mere object, he might have seen her desire to rise from the gutter by any means at hand as understandable, and he might have recognized that unlike men, women had no access to power other than through sex. All these implications are inherent in the situations in the novel, but Zola does not emphasize them. Rather, he creates a character who is destined to act as she does, and then he condemns her. In the middle of the novel, the journalist Fauchery publishes an article on Nana entitled "The Golden Fly" so similar to Zola's description of her in his *ébauche* that it seems to express the author's opinion directly:

> it was the story of a girl descended from four or five generations of drunkards, her blood tainted by an accumulated inheritance of poverty, and drink, which in her case had taken the form of a nervous derangement of the sexual instinct. She had grown up in the slums, in the gutters of Paris; and now, tall and beautiful, and as well made as a plant nurtured on a dungheap, she was avenging the paupers and outcasts of whom she was the product. With her the rottenness that was allowed to ferment among the lower classes was rising to the surface and

rotting the aristocracy. She had become a force of nature, a
ferment of destruction, unwittingly corrupting and disor-
ganizing Paris between her snow-white thighs, and cur-
dling it just as women every month curdle milk. It was at
the end of the article that the comparison with a fly
occurred, a fly the color of sunshine which had flown up
out of the dung, a fly which had sucked death from the
carrion left by the roadside and now, buzzing, dancing,
and glittering like a precious stone, was entering palaces
through the windows and poisoning the men inside, simply by settling on them (p. 221).

Such words as "blood tainted," "rottenness," "ferment of destruction," and "poisoning" indicate Zola's distaste for Nana,
but he does not dwell as much on the inference that she, the
fly, could not flourish or even exist if the "dungheap" and
"carrion" were cleared away. He says that Nana and those like
her are rotting the aristocracy, presumably by tempting them
into decadence through their animal instincts. But Zola does
not pursue here the question of who caused the "rottenness
that was allowed to ferment among the lower classes." Was it
not these same aristocrats whose wealth had been accumu-
lated at the expense of the poor?

In "The Human Fly," Zola reaffirms the notion that Nana
is bred to act as she does, and he posits a kind of class context
for her actions in that she is taking revenge on the aristocracy
for their exploitation of the proletariat. But she is not conscious of such a motivation, acting rather from instinct. And
when she does transfer the wealth of some aristocrats to
herself, she does not redistribute that wealth among the class
which produced her, at least not intentionally; instead, she
wastes it and is robbed by her own servants, thus completing
the cycle of ruthlessness, greed, and exploitation seen elsewhere in this dark condemnation of Second Empire society.

In *Nana*, then, prostitution becomes a metaphor for
Zola's view of sexuality. He, like many people in the last half
of the nineteenth century, felt that women did not feel sexual

desire as men did. When they did manifest passion, it was somehow degrading, as in Sabine Muffat's affair with Fauchery, or perverted, as in Nana's passion for young Georges Hugon when he puts on her dress. While Zola is correct in his assumption that prostitution does not provide sexual pleasure for a woman, he is unable to conceive of any situation in which passion in women is right and proper. When he depicts Nana as truly in love, it is with the brute Fontan, whose beatings and sadistic exploitation of Nana show that her love is really the female's desire for domination by the stronger male. Finally, Zola demonstrates throughout the novel a fundamental terror of the power of female sexuality and the complete ruin brought on men intent on its pursuit.

Zola also uses prostitution as a metaphor to depict the decay that led to the collapse of the Second Empire. To Zola, prostitution is emblematic of the purposelessness, selfishness, and immorality of the whole society, as he shows by the prostitute's ability to break up ancient families and ancient estates to indulge her childish greed. Pursuit of fulfillment for the libido through prostitution also betokens religious decline (Muffat's loss of faith), economic corruption (Steiner's embezzling), and political decay (the prince's courtship of Nana and the fall of the government). As the productions at the Théâtre des Variétés show, the arts, too, have been corrupted by sex. Nana's hideous death among courtesans who bring their kindness and concern too late parallels the simultaneous death of the Second Empire. Underlying it all is Zola's unmistakable hatred of women, whose full humanity he will not grant, choosing instead to place their total being in their genitalia. Although there is not a single positive character in the novel, and the men are as fallen as the women, the men have the redeeming moral value of being victims, while women, as victimizers, are one giant step lower on the ladder of morality.

The Magic Circle:
The Role of the Prostitute in
Isak Dinesen's Gothic Tales

THOMAS WHISSEN

THE WAY OPPOSITES define each other and thus give each other identity is one of Isak Dinesen's favorite themes. To her, opposites are "locked caskets, of which each contains the key to the other."[1] Such roles as husband, master, teacher, jailer, and artist do not exist independently; they come into being only in conjunction with their partners: wife, servant, pupil, prisoner, and audience. Throughout her tales Dinesen returns again and again to these exclusive partnerships, fascinated by the way they form a mystical and inviolable union, a "magic circle," as it were, within which they thrive and acquire meaning.

Dinesen, like Yeats, doubts the efficacy of that obsessive twentieth-century diversion, the search for individual identity, finding it, in Yeats's words, a "source of passivity and melancholy." Only in the contractual agreement established by the marriage of opposites and in strict observance of the conditions imposed by that agreement can identity be discovered and the individual life take on meaning. One becomes a willing and faithful participant in the duet of interdependent forces, and by playing one's part loyally and unswervingly, one is behaving with what Dinesen calls chivalrousness, which means "to love, or cherish, the pride of your partner, or of your adversary, as you will define it, as highly, or higher than, your own."[2]

Dinesen illustrates the nature of this quality of chivalrousness in "The Old Chevalier" from *Seven Gothic Tales* by focusing on the age-old relationship between prostitute and client. In this story it is made quite clear that the bargain the partners strike determines not only the roles they will play but also the way they will play them. Moreover, the contract between them is seen as a liberating rather than a restraining force because it allows the players to don a mask and thus enjoy all the freedom a disguise permits. To Dinesen's way of thinking, chivalrousness is a principle, and one's natural inclination is to submit to a principle. To refuse to submit is to thwart one's natural inclinations and thereby forfeit one's freedom and identity. To submit willingly and with good grace is to release one's natural inclinations and thereby attain freedom and identity.

Interestingly enough, the story of the prostitute and her client is told by the client, Baron von Brackel (the old chevalier) as his way of resolving the conflict between inclination and principle. In the introduction to this story, the baron, now an old man, is involved in a discussion with a young friend as to "whether one is ever likely to get any real benefit, any lasting moral satisfaction, out of forsaking an inclination for the sake of principle" (p. 81). This was a controversy dear to the hearts of the Romantics (cf. Schiller on *Pflicht* versus *Neigung*), and Dinesen sets out in this story, as she does elsewhere, to settle the matter by reconciling inclination and principle in the single impulse she labels chivalrousness.

The old chevalier is well aware that inclinations are not always natural (i.e., right). To be natural, they must be in spontaneous alignment with principle. The trouble is that it takes a flawless character to behave with such spontaneity.

THE MAGIC CIRCLE 45

Flawed humankind has to learn spontaneity and resist the temptation to let inclination and principle diverge or, worse yet, converge and thus dissolve. This is the lesson, if it can be called that, which the old chevalier teaches his young friend as he recounts this episode from his youth and the lesson he learned from the way in which the prostitute respects the bargain they have made.

The baron begins his story in classic Dinesen fashion:

> On a rainy night in the winter of 1874, on an avenue in Paris, a drunken young girl came up and spoke to me. I was then, as you will understand, quite a young man. I was very upset and unhappy, and was sitting bareheaded in the rain on a seat along the avenue because I had just parted from a lady whom, as we said then, I did adore, and who had within this last hour tried to poison me (p. 92).

It turns out that both the baron and his mistress had thought more highly of her husband than they had of each other, and the three-way jealousies that ensued had paralyzed any natural inclinations and made a mockery of principle. The baron found himself engaged in one of life's deadliest games, "the old game of the cat and the mouse—probably the original model of all the games of the world" (p. 84). His problem is that he finds out almost too late just what game he has been playing. Unholy alliance that it is, he sees it as the logical consequence of inclinations that have been perverted by dishonesty. Implicit in the narrative is his realization that ignorance of the rules and of one's own motives and obligations leads to moral damnation. Salvation lies in allegiance to principle through regenerated inclination. Neither he nor his mistress played fair with each other. He concealed his esteem for her husband, yet he complains that "exactly what she wanted me for I did not know" (p. 84). Suspecting that there had once been werewolves among her family, he thinks: "I should have been happier to see her really go down on all fours and snarl at me, for then I should have known where I was" (p. 84).

He knows where he is when the drunken young girl approaches him on that wintry night in Paris. The rules of her game are simple and well defined. What he does not yet know is that the rules are also exacting and are not to be tampered with. Even though she seems "like a person out on a great adventure, or someone keeping a secret" (p. 91), he is strangely not inclined to interfere with the role she has chosen. This unexpected reaction puzzles him. "If I had been normally balanced," he says, "I suppose I should have tried to get from her some explanation of the sort of mystery that she seemed to be, but now I do not think that this occurred to me at all" (p. 91). He is just beginning to realize that he is accepting his own role automatically, that a sense of partnership has sprung up between them. To his own surprise, he perceives her as some sort of gift and feels "a great happiness, a warmth" (p. 92). He senses that "something special and more than natural has been sent to him" (p. 92). He is succumbing to unreflecting impulse, to natural inclination, and when he gets her to his lodgings and gently removes her wet clothes, the act transcends the merely sensual to become mystically symbolic.

Without being conscious of it, the baron has surrendered to ritual, and as he performs his part in the ritual, he finds that the emptiness with which the recent encounter with his mistress left him is being filled with warmth and love. "Reality," he says, "had met me such a short time ago, in such an ugly shape, that I had no wish to come into contact with it again. Somewhere in me a dark fear was still crouching, and I took refuge within the fantastic like a distressed child in his book of fairy tales" (p. 98). As long as the two of them are in disguise and playing their parts, reality is suspended. "I did not want to look ahead," he says, "and not at all to look back. I felt the moment close over me, like a wave" (p. 98).

Safe within the bonds of their union, the young baron understands for the first time the sanctity of the compact he has entered into, and he is grateful. "My heart was filled with a very sweet gratitude . . . that the great friendly power of the universe should manifest itself again, and send me, out of the night, as a help and consolation, this naked and drunk young girl, a miracle of gracefulness" (p. 98). He also feels liberated. "I have never in any other love affair," he says, "had the same feeling of freedom and security. In my last adventure I had all the time been worrying to find out what my mistress really thought of me, and what part I was playing in the eyes of the world. But no such doubts or fears could possibly penetrate into our little room here. I believe that this feeling of safety and perfect freedom must be what happily married people mean when they talk about the two being one" (p. 99).

However, doubts intrude. Inclination, corrupted by skepticism, is suspicious of happiness. In the middle of the night, the baron awakes feeling that "something is wrong, is dangerous" (p. 101). He has fears that intervene. "I am to pay for this," he thinks, "what am I to pay?" (p. 101). So begins the temptation to violate the unwritten rules of the game he and the prostitute have been playing. Reality, the world of fears and doubts, has begun to dissipate the enchantment of their encounter. Consequently, he is not prepared to answer spontaneously, to listen to his natural inclinations, when, in the morning, as she is about to leave, the prostitute says: "And you will give me twenty francs, will you not?" (p. 102).

Fortunately, because of his previous experience with his mistress, the moment is not lost on him. In a flash he realizes fully the nature of the dance, as it were, he has been dancing. "This was the end of the play," he thinks. "A rare jest had been offered me, and I had accepted it; now it was up to me to keep the spirit of our game until the end" (p. 102). Nevertheless, he tries to think of ways to keep her, to continue the relationship, to move it out of its present sphere and into something it was never meant to be. Again, however, memory of what happened before as a consequence of the violation of a contract revives to remind him of his obligation. He knows that to ask for money is what the prostitute's role demands of her, and that to pay is what is expected of him. "If I were to give her twenty francs," he thinks, "she might still be safe within the magic circle of her free and graceful and defiant spirit. It was I who was out of character" (p. 102).

By asking to be paid, the prostitute has lived up to her assumed role. She has, as he says, "called, during our few hours, on all the chivalrousness that I had in my nature" (p. 103). A bargain had been struck, and up until this moment both partners have honored it. To renege now would be to violate the whole charmed encounter. Out of respect for her pride, therefore, the baron gives her the twenty francs, knowing that at least for the time being, she will be safe within the magic circle that the interdependence of opposites creates.

As Dinesen would have it, then, life is given meaning and value within the magic circle of mutual respect. Because he comes to know this, the baron is able for a time to protect the young prostitute from reality, which he describes as "wasted as a burnt house" (p. 102). By honoring the roles each was cast in, he has bowed down before the "illusions and arts with which we try to transform our world" (p. 102).

The moment she is gone, the baron thinks of running after her, of persuading her, after all, to return with him and perpetuate their alliance, but he is initially prevented from doing this by the fact that he is naked. The necessity of putting on clothes before he chases after her reminds him again of the roles they have been playing and of his obligation to honor them. He realizes that there is no way he can continue a relationship with her short of negating the bargain they have just kept. Fearful as he is of what may happen to her, he knows that he would only contribute to her downfall if he were to step out of character and attempt to turn their professional encounter into something personal. Out of respect for her integrity, he forsakes the inclination to rescue her, aware in that moment of choice that it is the only right thing to do and that it is a gesture that under ideal circumstances should have occurred to him spontaneously.

When he reflects on this incident later, the baron is convinced that a catastrophe of an extraordinarily violent nature has destroyed the girl, for he is now fully aware of the schism between inclination and principle and the difficult necessity of healing that schism. Who, he wonders, "would have valued her rare beauty, grace, and charm" (p. 104), who is there who would have cherished her pride higher than his own? "She must have gone straight down from the world of beauty and harmony," he thinks, "to a world where beauty and grace are of no account, and where the facts of life look you in the face, quite straight to ruin, desolation and starvation" (pp. 104–105).

Fifteen years later, in the studio of an artist friend, the baron comes upon the skull of a young woman. "I had it in my hand," he says, "and as I was looking at the broad, low brow, the clear and noble line of the chin, and the clean deep sockets of the eyes, it seemed suddenly familiar to me" (p. 107). Contemplating the skull, the sight of which inexplicably transports him back to that evening fifteen years earlier, he thinks of the polished bone shining so purely in the lamplight as "safe." He does not ask his friend about the identity of the skull because he is convinced that his friend would know nothing about it. The identity, of course, does not really matter. What matters is that the baron remembers, in the "safety" of that pure, white bone, another kind of safety he had known, perhaps only once, in the extraordinary evening he had spent with the young prostitute on that fateful night in 1874. They had met, he recalls, "in a special sort of sympathy" and had been in "quite a peculiar sort of mood, such as will hardly ever have repeated itself for either of us" (p. 91).

Students of German Romanticism will by now have noticed resemblances between Dinesen's "chivalrousness" and Schiller's *"schöne Seele"* and between the prostitute Nathalie in "The Old Chevalier" and the idealized Natalie of Goethe's *Wilhelm Meisters Lehrjahre,* a girl characterized in the novel as the embodiment of *die schöne Seele* (ideal person). In his essay, "On Dignity and Grace" *("Über Anmut und Würde"),* Schiller defines *die schöne Seele* as one whose instincts have been refined, whose emotions and irrationality have been ennobled to such an extent that he can entrust moral decisions even to the irrational aspect of his nature without running the risk of destroying the moral order by an unethical act. The Nathalie of the Dinesen story, described as "so innocent of heart," has indeed refined her instincts and ennobled her emotions, and it is these very qualities that inspire similar qualities in the young baron.

Just as Dinesen's chivalrousness is the reconciliation of inclination with principle, so is Schiller's *schöne Seele* the establishment of harmony between them, a harmony that to him can be brought about only by means of the interdependence of the beautiful and the ethical. Nathalie, described repeatedly as lovely, faultless, and graceful, enchants the baron with her "great sense of music" (p. 100) and the exquisite harmony between her body and her voice. Schiller believes that the harmony between inclination and duty is achieved through what he calls "play-instinct" *(Spieltrieb),* by which the instinctive is civilized rather than repressed. This sense of play pervades the entire scene between Nathalie and the baron as they laugh and tell stories, sing and sip champagne "high up there in my warm and quiet room, with the great town below us and my heavy silk curtains drawn upon the wet night, like two owls in a ruined tower within the depth of the forest" (p. 98).

One story Nathalie tells foreshadows her own fate at the hands of someone less chivalrous than the baron. It is about a "very old monkey which could do tricks, and had belonged to an Armenian organ-grinder. Its master had died, and now it wanted to do its tricks and was always waiting for the catchword, but nobody knew it" (p. 99). Only as long as her partner gives her the catchword can Nathalie continue to play her role, can the magic circle be preserved. As she tells the tale, she imitates the monkey "in the funniest and most gracefully inspired manner that one can imagine" (p. 99). The baron is in her thrall and thinks to himself "that the understanding of some pieces of music for violin and piano has come to me through the contemplation of the contrast, or the harmony, between her long slim hand and her short rounded chin as she held the glass to her mouth" (p. 99).

There is more of the geisha than the streetwalker in Dinesen's image of the prostitute. Nathalie, inexperienced though she is, is thoroughly "professional" because she is apprentice to her finest instincts. In her obedience to the laws of myth, in the spontaneous appropriateness of her behavior, she comes—and Dinesen says as much—to symbolize woman at ease with her own mystery and strangely empowered by it. She takes pride in the role she plays, and she expects others to cherish that pride as highly as she cherishes theirs.

The Romantization of
the Prostitute
in Dostoevsky's Fiction*

NICHOLAS MORAVCEVICH

NOTING THAT one of the contributors to Dostoevsky's journal *Vremja* called on contemporary Russian
writers to produce some "stories of the life of prostitutes,
honestly told with all the details and with psychological indi-
cations,"[1] Donald Fanger concluded that "Dostoevsky,
whether deliberately or not, did answer this call: after Liza in
Notes from the Underground came Sonia; and after the kept
women, Nastasia Filippovna and Grusenka."[2]

While the very breadth of Dostoevsky's interest in this
feminine archetype might readily suggest that he indeed ade-
quately covered its most significant variants, a closer perusal of
his works clearly reveals that he was far more interested in, and
from the sociological point of view far more successful with, the
portraiture of alluring, almost-respectable kept women than
with that of their lower-level sisters, the common streetwalkers
and brothel girls. The latter usually appear in his fiction as
greatly idealized, passive, meek creatures, melodramatically
prone to suffering and sacrifice and thus intrinsically quite

*The article first appeared in *Russian Literature* 4 (1976), 299–307. Reprinted by
permission of *Russian Literature*.

different from what that anonymous contributor to *Vremja* looked for when he suggested that the prostitutes in fiction should be presented so that the fullest circumstances of their existence would appear "honestly told with all the details."

On the whole, Dostoevsky's rendering of the fallen woman clearly suggests that in this sphere he remained solidly indebted to the traditions of the Western Gothic novel. Gogol, who translated some of these, as George Siegel noted, perceived the prostitute quite romantically and in a certain "vague and cloudy way, which seems typical of his descriptions of women in general."[3] The line from Gogol to Dostoevsky, however, was not a direct one since a number of Western romanticists and particularly Victor Hugo continued to influence Russian literature with numerous variations on the basic themes of the prostitute with a heart of gold and the prostitute rehabilitated. Not surprisingly, this quickly prompted the appearance of many native endeavors on the same subjects. Thus, Nekrasov, for example, in 1845 published his rhetorically sentimental poem "When from thy error, dark, degrading"[4] that obviously was inspired by Hugo's much earlier (1835) rhapsodical outcry, *"Oh! n'insultez jamais une femme qui tombe!"*[5] and in 1864, Vsevolod Krestovsky followed with a gushingly sentimental story, "A Dear but Fallen Creature,"[6] which told of love between an impressionable student and a secretly debauched but outwardly angelic fallen woman that was quite reminiscent of Hugo's virtuous prostitutes such as Paquette in *Notre-Dame de Paris* (1831) and Fantine in *Les Misérables* (1862).

Since this particular story appeared in the first number of Dostoevsky's periodical *Epocha* (1864), Siegel is again quite correct in concluding that "although today Krestovsky's story seems hopelessly banal, trite and sentimental, Dostoevsky, in selecting it for the first issue of his new journal . . . must have considered it a serious contribution to the problem of the fallen woman."[7]

Sociologically, however, the most valid rendering of the prostitute and the process of her rehabilitation in this entire era appeared in Cernysevsky's novel-treatise *What Is to Be Done?*, published approximately a year before Dostoevsky's *Epocha* brought out the story of Krestovsky. In Cernysevsky's work, the love affair between the medical student Kirsanov and the brothel girl Kryukova is allowed to develop gradually through several authentically realistic stages, each utterly devoid of either Gogolesque mystery or Nekrasovian rhetoric. In discussing her brothel days, for example, Kryukova quite matter of factly admits that

> I was a very wicked girl, Vera Pavlovna. . . . And I was very insolent; I had no shame, and was always drunk. . . . As to the life that I led, of course there is no occasion to speak of it; it is always the same with poor women of that sort.[8]

The love of Kirsanov and Kryukova is, of course, not the main subject of Cernysevsky's novel but merely an episode in the larger whole intended to be a launching vehicle for the author's progressive social ideas. Since it was precisely the critique of these ideas as well as the ideas of sentimental humanitarianists like Nekrasov that prompted Dostoevsky to write his *Notes from the Underground* in 1864, he naturally did not fail to introduce in this work his own version of an encounter between a young man and a prostitute that was in several ways satirically juxtaposed to Cernysevsky's novel.

Both Cernysevsky's Kryukova and Dostoevsky's Liza are brothel girls. Both are in some way entangled with medical students, both are tubercular, and both are shown in two separate encounters with their patrons. But while Kryukova is helped by Kirsanov to pay her debts, leave the brothel, and achieve a measure of independence and tranquility, Liza is first given some such hope by the underground man during their initial tête-à-tête in the brothel and then is ravished, abused, and cruelly insulted by him when in response to his invitation she arrives at his shabby lodgings expecting that his previous outburst of humanitarian concern for her and her future was more than empty scheming, rhetoric.

As Viktor Sklovsky has already pointed out,[9] it is true that the plot development of Notes from the Underground clearly indicates that Dostoevsky wanted to permeate his work with a distinctly antiromantic flavor. But it is also true that in the second part of this piece, "Apropos of the Wet Snow," in which the straight monolog of the first part slowly evolves into something more akin to the narrative of a conventional novel, he succeeds in this only partially. All the satire and parody of progressive views and sentimental humanitarianism that can be detected in the underground man and in the Liza episode distinctly emanate from the verbal posturing and psychological perturbations of our mockingly anti-heroic protagonist, the underground man. Poor Liza is but a target and a sounding board for her partner's antics; even the base rascal himself is surprised at the extent of her naiveté and gullibility when he recollects her reaction to both the content and tone of his brothel tirade:

> "Yes, that's only to be expected from these stupid, pure-hearted romantics! Ah, damn them, these filthy, stupid, rotten, sentimental souls! How could she have failed to see through it all?"... "And how few words it took," I noted. "How little of an idyll—especially since it wasn't even a real idyll, but a literary contrivance—it took to turn a whole human soul upside down in less than a minute. That's girlish innocence for you! That's virgin soil!"[10]

Although Liza is Dostoevsky's prime example of a brothel girl, nothing that he lets us know about her background, appearance, behavior, or aspirations in any way indicates even the slightest degree of professional deformation. In clear contrast with the underground man's monumental conceit and hysterical irritability, she seems to possess an infinite reserve of kindness, humility, and intuitive understanding of others, although objectively speaking, a situation as degrading as that in which she finds herself here would in reality hardly elicit from anyone such a meek and sentimental response to insults and abuse. Consequently, while the successful rendering of the true-to-life portrait of the underground man enabled Dostoevsky to expose and ridicule many saccharine platitudes on the subject of the fallen woman expressed by his numerous literary predecessors and contemporaries, his simultaneous failure to desentimentalize the character of Liza as well blunted some of his own satirical edge. Thus, ultimately, his own work retains much of the sentimental undertone that bothered him in the works of contemporary liberals, since the grossly deceived and insulted Liza (whose trustfulness and naiveté are deliberately highlighted so that her antagonist can trample on them) ultimately emerges so exalted that she herself readily becomes a new romantic symbol of the fallen woman, this one of Dostoevsky's own creation.

In fact, this is doubly true, for Liza appears to be just as much a character of the underground man's own making, since she is wholly his invention. From the standpoint of the narrative technique, *Notes from the Underground* is an uninterrupted reminiscence of its hero; thus, all the information that reaches the reader about Liza and her actions is available only through the medium of the recollection and confession of the underground man himself. Consequently, it is pointless to envisage and analyze the encounter of the underground man and Liza as an actual event or an objectively described happening (as some notable critics have done),[11] for nothing is further from the truth. If there is anything that the underground man is for, it is the absolute freedom to perceive and interpret every segment of reality as he pleases. Since we know how smugly and morbidly proud he is of his odiousness, dualism, and inconsistency (his personality traits, which were labeled by Robert Lord as demoniacal in the truest Kierkegaardian sense, include "an exaggerated sensibility, an exaggerated irritability, nervous affections, hysteria, hypochondria, etc."[12]), all his statements about Liza's actions and all his explanations of the motives behind them are obviously self-serving and therefore, objectively speaking, unreliable.

As Dostoevsky's best known example of a streetwalker, Sonia Marmeladova represents an even clearer case of deliberate sentimentalization, since the "exaltation of the fallen woman, which is implicit in Notes from the Underground, becomes an outright apotheosis in Crime and Punishment."[13] Only the brief description of Sonia's dress in the scene of her father's death, which is her first appearance in the novel, gives the reader some clue as to her true occupation:

> She was also dressed in rags; her attire was trashy, but it was tricked out in street fashion according to the taste and rules prevailing in that particular world of hers, and directed toward one glaringly and shamefully conspicuous end. She stepped on the landing . . . conscious, it seemed of nothing, having forgotten about her fourth-hand, flowery silk dress that was indecent here, with its immensely long, ridiculous train and vast crinoline, blocking the whole door, and forgetting also her brightly colored boots, the parasol that she had brought with her, though it was useless at night, and her ridiculous, round straw hat with a bright scarlet feather in it.[14]

Everything else that Dostoevsky says in the novel about her is utterly contrary to what ordinarily might be expected in a portrait of a common streetwalker. In complete contradiction to that corrupting pull of gutter existence which Dostoevsky elsewhere in the novel depicts with a naturalistic veracity equal to Zola's best endeavor, Sonia is presented as a wholly unspoiled, innocent, shy, and trustworthy soul. She is a prostitute who throughout the novel is neither shown in a degrading soliciting situation nor exposed as at least to some degree behaviorally harmed by her early fall into disrepute. In fact, she is thrust upon the reader with such an idealistic bias that even the very suggestion of the taint of her body seems to accentuate the strength of her spiritual purity and faith in goodness. While this emphasis on her spirit correctly prompted Simmons to conclude that she "is a kind of living universal symbol of crushed and suffering humanity that bears within itself the undying seed of joyous resurrection,"[15] it also must not be forgotten that the very presence in this case of Dostoevsky's intentional contrast of such gross opposites as the profanity of the flesh and the saintliness of the spirit is a distinctly Romantic device.

In order not to destroy anything of this firm idealistic foundation of Sonia's character, Dostoevsky was particularly careful not to encumber her and Raskolnikov's relationship with even the faintest hint of physical attraction or familiarity. Such jottings as "there is not a word of love between them. This is a *sine qua non,*"[16] which reappear throughout his notes on *Crime and Punishment,* strongly suggest that he deliberately aimed to contrast the naturalistic ambience of the shabby Saint Petersburg streets with the sentimentally chaste, ascetic relationship of the two bizarre urban characters, much of whose activity is romantically defined in terms of heightened moments of either transgression or atonement. Consequently, Siegel's assertion that "the portrait of Sonia Marmeladova teeters precariously on the edge of sentimentality,"[17] does not really go far enough, since such an understatement hardly shows that the Romantic ethos pervades the very core of Sonia's personality.

It has been noted already that Liza from *Notes from the Underground* exists only through the underground man's recollection, for only his interpretation of the aim and meaning of her actions and reactions is known to us. Interestingly enough, Fanger perceives a similar pattern in Sonia's relationship with Raskolnikov when he notes that "Sonia, for instance, is seen only in his company, only in reaction to him and through his reaction to her."[18] This too underscores the extent of the romantic element in the portraiture of Sonia, since by keeping her away from the personages and events that gave the novel its realistic and even naturalistic flavor, Dostoevsky managed to sketch her without the stylistic compromises he would have had to make otherwise. In this way Dostoevsky in effect successfully outdid even his romantic-realist predecessors, for in his hands their conventional theme of the prostitute with a heart of gold was elevated readily into that of the prostitute sanctified.

That the overidealized image of the fallen woman in Dostoevsky's fiction is one of the most vivid examples of his ties with the urban Gothic tradition of his romantic-realist predecessors was also well perceived by George Steiner when he noted that "behind the figure of Sonia we may discern that of 'little Ann' of Oxford Street."[19] This, however, is only a partial answer, for this tendency to make his characters larger than life was also the inevitable outcome of Dostoevsky's rare ability to internalize conflict and magnify the most minute details in any psychological relationship. Although this technique helped him augment the stature and significance of all his characters, such magnification with his best examples of the kept woman, Nastasia Filippovna and Grusenka, greatly buttressed both the psychological and social authenticity of the portraiture, while with his best examples of the prostitute, Liza and Sonia Marmeladova, it frequently strained the social veracity of the resultant portraits.

Yet when it came to the lesser characters who lurk in the seedy background of his urban milieu, Dostoevsky occasionally could, when his artistic aims permitted it, produce a sketch of a fallen woman with all the naturalistic veracity of the camera eye. Such is his depiction of the old prostitute whom the underground man invents to frighten Liza and thus subjugate her to his will:

Once—it was on a New Year's morning—I saw a woman there by the door of a house. Her own colleagues had pushed her out as a practical joke—to cool her off for a while because she was bawling—then they decided to lock the door on her. So, at nine in the morning, there she was, completely drunk, unkept, half naked, badly beaten. There was a thick layer of powder on her face, still black bruises under both eyes, and blood streaming from her nose and mouth. Some cabby had just dealt with her, it seems. She sat on the doorstep bewailing her "miseries" at the top of her voice, striking the steps with a salt herring she held in her hand, as a bunch of drunken soldiers and cabbies gathered around her and taunted her.[20]

The old hag sketched here is also a spectral creature like Liza, for she too is but an unverifiable memory in the fickle, tantrum-prone, malignant mind of the underground man. However, far more real as a cameo picture of a common prostitute is the minor episode in *Crime and Punishment* in which the delirious Raskolnikov runs into a young streetwalker, Duklida. After she brazenly takes his last few kopecks for a drink and promises to reward his generosity with all her charms at some later time, she quickly disappears both from her beat and from the novel's narrative so that anything about her beyond that which is seen in this vignette simply remains unknown. Had she, however, for some reason been destined to reappear and assume a more significant part in the novel's action, it is most likely that the power of Dostoevsky's imagination and his rare gift for intense psychological magnification of any facet of commonplace reality would have molded her into a character whose behavior and personality traits would be as unusual and idealized as those of Liza and Sonia. That Dostoevsky was not very much disturbed that such an approach to characterization might be vestigially romantic is clear from one of his letters to Strachov, in which he said: "I have my own view of art, and that which the majority call fantastic and exceptional is for me the very essence of reality."[21]

The Prostitute in Arab
and North African Fiction

EVELYNE ACCAD

A NUMBER OF WRITERS from North Africa and the Arab world have dealt with the problem of prostitution in their novels, sometimes as a central theme (Mahfūz and Djebar) and sometimes indirectly (Memmi, Jabra, and Boudjedra). The writers selected here represent a wide range of countries. Jabra Ibrahim Jabra is originally Palestinian but lives in Iraq; he writes in English and Arabic. Naguib Mahfūz is an Egyptian who writes in Arabic. Albert Memmi is a Tunisian Jew who now lives in Paris and writes in French. Rachid Boudjedra and Assia Djebar are both Algerian and write in French; they live both in Paris and in Algeria.

Before discussing the image of the prostitute in the novels written by these five authors, it is important to look briefly at the literature from North Africa and the Arab world and examine some of its characteristics. It is also important to trace the problem of prostitution within the context of the overall condition of oppression of Arab and North African women as reflected in the novels and in society.

If there is a single literary characteristic which can be said to exist throughout most of the novels from these two areas, it is probably the distinctive narrative stance. Many of the works

63

are narrated in the first person, and most have a certain autobiographical element. Taken together, these two characteristics give to most of these works a quality of immediacy and urgency. One finds virtually no sense of calm detachment, of full and intricate exploitation of the reflective possibilities of the third-person omniscient mode.

In many ways, the contemporary fiction of North Africa and the Arab world reflects the prevailing technical and stylistic tendencies of fiction in other parts of the world. It should be remembered that much of the cultural context of these writers is exogenous: They are often in more intimate contact with the language and society of Europe than they are with their own. From the almost quaint romanticism of Haykal to the Saganism of the early Djebar, one notes many examples of "native" subject matter treated in terms of "foreign" literary conventions.

Critics approaching this body of literature should remember that they are dealing with a literary tradition that is quite literally in its infancy. Arabic fiction (at least in the Western sense), for instance, cannot be traced back beyond Haykal at the beginning of World War I, while the Francophone literature of North Africa appears only after World War II. As such, a great deal of this literature is necessarily tentative and experimental, often involving the adaptation of existing literary techniques to a set of cultural conditions which exist nowhere else in the world.

Some of these cultural elements are the Moslem religious heritage and a history of European colonial domination, usually at the hands of the French or the English. Islam leaves its mark in many ways that the Western reader is likely to regard as being outside the purview of religion. There is, for instance, little or no distinction between religious and civil law; codes based on Koranic injunctions and centuries of religious practice often suffice for both purposes. The three religions— Islam, Christianity, and Judaism—which originated from that part of the world have all tended traditionally to provide extensive and explicit guidelines for daily living. It is in large part from these religious customs that the social and legal treatment of women has been shaped.

The second cultural element created a biocultural stress by means of the intrusion of a colonial presence which runs deep beneath many of the works to be discussed here. With the Algerian writers it is particularly clear that this biculturality bears strongly on the question of the condition of women. Not only does the alien European culture provide new behavior patterns for the North African woman to adopt, the native reaction against colonial domination often leads to the rigorous reinstatement of traditional restrictions on women, generally in the name of Arab nationalism.

On the other hand, various socioeconomic factors can be seen to vary markedly from country to country. Literacy rates, per capita income, and the range of government social services often differ greatly, even in neighboring countries. These contrasting conditions cause certain shifts in the literary emphasis of works originating in these areas. Thus, while certain of the Iraqi and Algerian writers deal with the condition of women at the level of bare biological survival, one finds writers from more literate countries such as Egypt and Lebanon to be more concerned with the problems that arise from upward social, economic, and educational mobility.

In critical terms, it is meaningless to talk of the success or failure of literature in capturing the sociological realities on which it is based. When, however, one's concern is to measure the social impact and relevance of a particular literature, it is fruitful to compare literary and sociological perceptions of the real world; the nature of the transformations which reality undergoes as it becomes fiction often says much about both the fictional process and the original reality.

The picture presented by a sociological examination of the life of the Arab woman is a haunting one. Often unwelcome at birth, sometimes circumcised, mostly uneducated, cloistered, told that her virginity is so precious that her brothers are ready to kill her if she loses it, the Arab girl moves toward maturity. At an early age she is the unwitting and often unwilling partner in an arranged marriage. On the wedding night, tradition demands the satisfaction of the husband, with no thought given to the fear, pain, or sexual immaturity of the thirteen- to sixteen-year-old bride. After this often brutal sexual initiation, the young girl is required to bring into the world as many children (preferably male) as possible, with no regard for her health. Frequently she must share her husband with other women without having comparable sexual privileges. The servitude implicit in her social role allows her to be beaten at her husband's whim and divorced at his convenience. She must obey his commands without question and bear oppression by his mother without complaint. Often she goes through life without ever having known a fullness of freedom and choice, mental or physical self-fulfillment, or the satisfaction of choosing and achieving her own goals.

The novels written by the Arab and North African male novelist depict these many sides of oppression suffered by women in Arabo-Islamic societies. In depicting the suffering that occurs through the absence of personal freedoms, these writers describe women in various relationships: familial (wife, mother, sister, aunt, grandmother) and illicit (adulterous mistress, concubine, prostitute, slave, servant). The fact that these relationships are almost invariably defined by the nature of a woman's connection with a man indicates the extreme degree to which the social status of Arab women is both male-centered and male-sanctioned. The condition of women being what it is in these societies, prostitution is only one further level of degradation.

This essay will look briefly at five novels dealing with or portraying prostitution: Memmi's *The Salt Statue*, Boujedra's *The Repudiation*, Mahfūz *Midāq Alley*, Jabra's *Hunters in a*

Narrow Street, and Djebar's *The Naive Larks.* The first four
novelists are men, and the last is a woman.

In *La Statue de sel (The Salt Statue,* Paris, 1953), the
women of the *quartier réservé* are used by Albert Memmi to
depict the dehumanization of women in his culture. Within
the novel, Mordekhai's (the hero and the author himself)
involvement with the prostitutes signifies the shift in his life
from adolescence to manhood. Mordekhai's vivid descriptions of the women of the *quartier réservé* hold the same
nostalgia for him as the memory of Ginou, his first flirt; both
are mixed with a certain sadness and disgust.

The first to initiate Mordekhai sexually is a small,
chubby woman dressed in blue who stares at the ceiling
during the whole sexual act. She is an automaton, repeating
the same set of gestures every fifteen minutes. Mordekhai goes
into his first sexual experience awkwardly and with embarrassment. He is not even sure how to offer payment. When he
tells the prostitute that she is his first woman, she only smiles
faintly. Coming out of the *quartier,* Mordekhai is ashamed of
himself. He feels dirty, "a prostitute himself," "an accomplice
in this misery," and degraded. Nevertheless, he goes back and
gets used to the fact that the women often talk or smoke while
he takes his pleasure. He expresses the loneliness awakened in
him by the *quartier réservé:* "O, the loneliness of love in the
bordello! This is why all my friends would talk about it
among themselves: to break this loneliness in front of the
woman."[1] This loneliness seems to represent yet another aspect
of the oppression of women in North African society: Prostitution reinflicts the loneliness and degradation on the men,
who become mere customers to be served.

The second novel seems more overtly concerned with
making a satirical statement about society as a whole. Rachid
Boudjedra in *La Répudiation (The Repudiation,* Paris, 1969)
describes the prostitutes in many passages that reveal the
double standards and hypocrisy of his society. The whole

novel is a plea against the conditions under which the women of his country suffer, starting with repudiation (as the title of the book indicates) and culminating with prostitution.

As a young boy, the narrator remembers *Ramadhan*, the Moslem month of fasting, when fasting was equivalent to feasting because the whole clan (extended family) would indulge at night in whatever they did not have during the day. The visit to the mosque also meant a visit to the prostitutes, the holy building being so close to the prostitutes' quarter that the children walked right through it.[2] They witnessed their male adult relatives indulging in religious fervor followed by religious transgression. The double standards of the rich merchants of the city are made fun of by the narrator, who describes these men spending the long and hot nights of *Ramadhan* with luxury prostitutes (p. 35).

A scene with a prostitute sums up the feeling of revulsion and alienation the narrator experiences when confronting the condition of women in his country. He has gone to a prostitute who lives in a dirty room surrounded with pictures of women she has cut out of a nudist magazine. The prostitute lies down on the bed, waiting for the young man to get undressed. At the sight of her red vulva in the middle of hair and creases, spread above a filthy towel, with one of her tired breasts hanging out, he is filled with such disgust that he cannot have sex with her. He pays and leaves (p. 153).

Other images of prostitutes are given to enhance the overall descriptions of the condition of women and prostitutes. Early in the morning, when he has not yet fallen asleep because he is suffering from insomnia, he watches his neighbors running off to brothels, where "they risked the loss of their dignity and self-respect in front of fat prostitutes exciting them by plunging Coca-Cola bottles in their vaginas" (p. 200).

It is hard to differentiate between reality and delirium in this novel in which the young narrator, Boudjedra himself, exasperated by his society's abuses and treatment of women, goes into long descriptions of prostitutes and illicit and incestuous love affairs surrounded with violence, blood, fear, superstition, and puritanical hypocrisy. The harshest criticism goes to the father, who has strong moral and religious principles which allow him to repudiate his first wife (the narrator's mother) and marry three other young women consecutively. The father preaches against prostitution, alcohol, and bordellos, but the young child feels his mother's repudiation as a personal humiliation, which colors the rest of his life with a desire for revenge.

Perhaps more dramatic and a little more romanticized, the third novel reveals no less harsh a view of the prostitutes' condition. The most striking portrait in Naguib Mahfūz's novel *Zuqāq al-Meddaq* (*Midāq Alley*, Cairo, 1948) is that of Hamida, an orphan girl who becomes a prostitute. She is reared by a woman who is a bath attendant and marriage broker. Hamida's downfall is her desire to become part of the glittering, cash nexus world beyond the alley. To her, this cash-based freedom represents the only real life in Cairo, and these ambitions become the basis of her dealings with her potential suitors in the alley.

A strange young man who dresses like a European has appeared in the alley and makes overtures to Hamida. He perceives at once her desire for material things and knows exactly what promises to hold before her. She falls into his trap and, as might be expected, ends up as a prostitute, albeit in one of the best sections of Cairo. When 'Abbass, one of her suitors, returns from the military, he goes to find Hamida to bring her back. Unfortunately, her customers on that particular night are a group of British soldiers. A fight ensues, and 'Abbass is killed.

Although there is a mildly negative, tacit judgment of Hamida on the part of the author for her greed and her acceptance of things foreign to the alley, her downfall is described objectively rather than moralistically. Prostitution is not presented as totally vicious and corrupt; not only does it have its glamorous aspects, it represents an escape from poverty for Hamida. Indeed, the adoptive mother, Umm Hamida, is not above accepting loans from her daughter, the prostitute, in times of economic trouble.

Mahfūz' work is crowded with strong, middle-aged, middle-class women who are brash, loud, and bold. Some of his prostitutes belong to this category of virago women who play the role of mothers in prostitution, reinforcing Bouhdiba's thesis. One of these women, "the old guardian of the ladies" (Ajouzat al stut), is quite clear about it. She tells her client, "Your father was my lover. Tonight will be the night of your life."[3] The Freudian implications are obvious: By sleeping with the prostitute his father had slept with, he goes back into the womb, and on a different level, by possessing his mother, he gains victory over his father's power.

The next work to be discussed is more sensational and perhaps more personal than the others but seems to back away from a serious statement about the conditions it portrays. The prostitutes in Jabra Jabra's novel Hunters in a Narrow Street (London, 1960) are surrounded by an atmosphere of violence and tragedy in which the narrator shows his deep and even painful involvement in the fate of Middle Eastern society.

Jameel, the narrator, settles in Baghdad, where he has his first experience with Iraqi mores when he is searched for weapons by a policeman before being allowed to enter a redlight district. Later, his friends explain that he was searched because so many brothers go to the district to kill their sisters, who have become prostitutes, as a way of avenging the family honor.

His second experience is more violent. He returns to his hotel room one day and hears the screams of a woman rushing to his door. Yousef, the doorman of the hotel, a man the narrator had considered to be "a most gentle creature,"[4] is chasing her, armed with a knife which he plunges into her pregnant belly before the narrator can intervene. Yousef then bursts into tears: "It was his sister's abdomen he had ripped." At the same time, one of the spectators to the crime shouts to Yousef: "Is it a matter of honor? Well done, man!" The onlooker is a sheikh, and Adnān, one of Jameel's friends, whispers: "There is honor for you. Of course the honorable sheikh is on his way to visit a prostitute right now, but no matter" (p. 45). Adnān adds that Yousef will get at most a three- or four-year sentence for his sister's murder because "this was the only thing for him to do. If he hadn't done it he would have been the laughing stock of his family and friends." As Adnān puts it, "We live in cities and yet follow the law of the desert. We're caught in the vicious meshes of tribal tradition" (p. 46).

Along with the narrator, the reader is introduced immediately to the violence, double standards, hypocrisy, and despair which surround the lives of women in Baghdad. At the same time, however, there seems to be almost an air of comical resignation around these violent and oppressive customs. A friend of Jameel's who is a journalist reacts in a completely blasé manner to an account of the murder: "It's one of those repetitive things, you know. I shan't even bother to write a story about it for my paper. Now, had the girl been the murderess—well" (p. 48).

The only woman writer to have written extensively about the prostitute is Assia Djebar, a North African. The title of one of her novels, *Les Alouettes naïves (The Naive Larks, 1967)*, is the name the "legionnaires used for the prostitute-dancers of her country . . . symbol of outside degradation and inside light. . . . "[5] She says that in her country, newly freed Algeria, there are three categories of women: the cloistered wives of the harem, the prostitutes, and the heroines of the war, the fighting women. Men are afraid of the latter two categories but especially of the heroines of the war, with whom they do not know how to act (p. 235).

The image of the prostitute that Djebar gives us is very

different from the ones the male writers give. The Arab men describe the prostitutes as disgusting and repulsive and the relations they have had with them as detached and practical, in an atmosphere of violence, blood, rape, murder, and hypocritical double standards. Djebar, on the other hand, draws the image of a romantic love affair between two of her male characters, Rachid and his brother, and a prostitute, Meriem. The story is told by the brother.

Rachid takes his brother to the bordello, romantically described in the Casbah, the heart of the city "scented with spices and crushed mandarines . . . where multiple stairs marked the degree of its kneeling throughout the centuries" (p. 50). It is the brother's first sexual experience, and he has it with a prostitute, Meriem. ("Meriem" is a form of "Mary," like the Mary of the Bible or the Koran, indicating the virginal, pure aspect of the relationship.) Rachid wants his brother to have this prostitute specifically, and the narrator discovers that the reason for it is that Rachid had had a romantic relationship with her which he had cut short.

The only time Rachid goes back to Meriem is at the death of one of his relatives, Zhor (meaning "flower" in Arabic), who died as a result of her country's cruel treatment of women. She had been forced into a marriage at too young an age and had to produce children immediately, which resulted in her death in a miscarriage. In a rage, Rachid tells his brother: "Why did they insist? The doctor warned them. . . . She was given over for the reproduction of the Yacoub family . . . a machine factory for producing children," and then his voice breaks up in tears: "she was soft . . . soft! Do you remember her?" (p.82). That same day he goes to the bordello and asks for Meriem, whom he had been avoiding for a secret reason which his brother (the narrator) discovers only at Meriem's death.

After that visit, Meriem takes up drinking and dies of pleurisy in the narrator's arms. A few days earlier, when she was already agonizing, she had said to him: "I love you," and he had realized that those words were addressed to Rachid rather than to him.

Meriem's death follows Zhor's by barely six months. The two deaths have one thing in common: Both characters die as victims of the harsh conditions women suffer from in a society that dehumanizes them. They are both reduced to sexual objects: Meriem for the pleasure of the male of her society and Zhor for the reproduction of that same society. Neither one can achieve any degree of self-fulfillment or self-realization by living with the man she loves (Meriem) or by living in a marriage of her own choosing and need (Zhor).

When Rachid learns of Meriem's death, he decides to spend all his money to have prayers recited over her, and he confesses to his brother: "When I went to bed with her, she did not make me pay . . . she did not say anything but I knew I shouldn't propose anything to her. . . . We have to pay for her now, now that she will be sleeping with vermin" (p. 116).

His brother realizes that Rachid has understood something that other men in his country do not. For Rachid, the women of the bordello are the same as the women of his family. "Only Rachid, without analyzing the drama, had already guessed it, his instinct having always been sure. Only he skipped the barriers: going with the same identity, the same steps, the same assurance . . . from the bordello to the family home. . . . " Rachid is not split by a dialectal way of thinking, but "he had the behavior of a total and free man" (p. 88).

It is interesting to notice that the narrator in the novel is a man, Rachid's brother; of course, in reality it is Assia Djebar, an Algerian woman. Could a man have given us some of these descriptions of prostitutes with the same sensitivity and feeling of tenderness? The considerable difference between the descriptions of prostitutes in the novels by male authors and the one written by Djebar indicates the extreme alienation between men and women in Arabo-Islamic societies. By putting tender and romantic words for prostitutes into the mouth of a male character, Djebar cleverly tries to break some of these barriers. The *trotteuses* (trotters, from *trottoir*, a sidewalk, a slang word for prostitutes that here holds poetic qualities) move like white swallows who run underneath their white veils. The narrator feels tenderness for them as he did for Meriem, whom he considered as his bride, "a tenderness mixed with sadness, but above all a sort of complicity" (p. 232).

Prostitution has flourished and is still flourishing in most Arabo-Islamic societies. Throughout history, a few religious leaders have tried to do away with it and close the houses of prostitution, but reforms never lasted long, and prostitution soon reemerged in one form or another. Thus, despite the opposition of the state religion, prostitution has demonstrated that it has a definite function in society, for society has always found a place for it.

Yet Koranic law does allow men a variety of sexual pleasures: wives (up to four) and concubines (an unlimited number) as long as they are legally engaged in such activities. Whatever falls outside this legality is considered a sin *(zina)*, and *zina* is one of the worst offenses, punishable by death.

The Koran, however, is against prostitution *(bighā, khanā)*, which is outside the accepted contracts of sexuality, namely, marriage and concubinage *(nikāh)*. The Koranic injunctions against prostitution are clear: "Prosperous are the believers, who in their prayers are humble . . . and guard their private parts save from their wives and what their right hands own (concubines), then being not blame-worthy (but whosoever seeks after more than that, those are the transgressors),"[6] "and those who restrain their senses, except in respect of their wives and those under their control; such are not to blame, but those who seek to go beyond that are the transgressors."[7]

What then are some of the conditions in Arabo-Islamic

societies which have allowed prostitution to flourish? First, the societies are very repressive sexually, and prostitution allows a certain amount of freedom and releases part of the sexual tension of the men. Second, it provides a way out for men who cannot pay for the legal forms of sexuality *(nikāh)*. In most Arabo-Islamic societies, the Arab man has to pay a certain amount of money *(mahr)* in order to have a wife or a concubine. In any case, wives and concubines are more expensive to support than prostitutes. Third, according to Abdelwahab Bouhdiba, the sexual life of a young Arab male is taken in charge almost entirely by organized prostitution.[8] It is in the bordellos that young Arab males are initiated sexually before they get married.

The psychological implications of this form of sexuality take Oedipal proportions because of the age difference between the two groups: The males are young adolescents, and the prostitutes are usually in their forties. Also, according to Bouhdiba, the prostitute in this initiation of "love" is a substitute for the mother (p. 238). What Bouhdiba seems to forget is that in a sexual act such as prostitution, love does not play a great part. The presentation of prostitution in the novels helps make this very clear.

It also must be said that the male Arab writers considered here have managed to incorporate a substantial concern for the condition of prostitutes and women into their portrayal of their own anguish at the cultural and at times economic oppression in which they themselves were reared. That this is the case may suggest that the oppression of women seems to have nearly as marked an effect on the upbringing of the Arab male as it does on the women themselves. At times it is clearly evident that the oppressor is oppressed by his own oppression, and in any case the hypocrisy and double standards which result from the social code color much of the moral element of society. As in a Greek tragedy, it is impossible for society to escape the pollution of any of its members.

Courtesans and Prostitutes in South Asian Literature

ANN LOWRY WEIR

SEX AND MONEY are the two invariable items of exchange for both courtesans and prostitutes. South Asian writers have dealt with a varied array of women engaged in the "oldest profession," ranging from the beautiful and talented dancing girls of the emperors' courts to the starving, ragged derelicts who turn tricks in hopes of surviving from one day to the next. This study details and analyzes the roles of courtesans and prostitutes in a number of twentieth-century South Asian literary works in an effort to show a general pattern.

In classical and medieval India, courtesans were expected to act, sing, and dance. Extensive training and artistic ability as well as beauty were required. One early but still well-known portrayal of a compassionate and beautiful courtesan appears in the drama *Mrichchhakatika (The Little Clay Cart)* by the Sanskrit playwright Sudraka (ca. A.D. 500).[1] Even after political power passed to the Mughal emperors and later to the British East India Company and then to the British government, a few locales continued to maintain their centuries-old reputations for culture. Lucknow, a city in north-central India, was one of these. A lively and historically significant biographical novel concerning the life of a late-nineteenth-century Lucknawi courtesan is *Umrao Jan Ada (The Courtesan of Lucknow)*, by Mirza Ruswa. The courtesan's story is transcribed, we are told, almost directly by the author, who was one of the best Urdu prose writers of his day. Several editions of the book were snapped up by an eager audience soon after publication in 1905 —due in part, no doubt, to the risqué nature of the book's central character and theme.[2]

Lucknow's reputation as a cultural capital is aptly described in the introduction to a modern English translation of *The Courtesan of Lucknow:*

> The refined repartee of the people of Lucknow made other people's speech sound rustic; their polished manners made those of others appear oafish. It was the same with their way of living—their food, drink, and smoke. . . . All these excellent virtues were seen at their best in the establishments of courtesans where young aristocrats were sent to learn how to deport themselves—and incidentally also to learn the facts of life (pp. 12, 13).

If we believe that Umrao Jan (also known as Ada) candidly expressed her feelings to Ruswa, we come away from her biography with some interesting insights. She explains, for instance, that a courtesan finds a "kept man" to be "extremely useful." He shops for her, nurses her when she is ill, and helps "while away the time" between customers. "They praise their mistresses . . . entrap clients and persuade them to part with their cash. . . . When a girl picks up a rich patron, these people provide the element of rivalry" (p. 64). Thus, there is a clear difference between the relationship of a courtesan to her kept man and that of a common prostitute to her pimp. The courtesan, whose reputation is based on her own talents, is clearly in control of her own situation and income.

Twilight in Delhi (1940) concerns life among the Indian capital's Muslim elite during the second decade of this century. Ahmed Ali evokes the city's mood during a period of transition from old ways to new, with the advent of World War

I and the almost simultaneous rise of the Indian National Congress and Mahatma Gandhi's noncooperation movement. Mir Nihal, one of the novel's main characters, has a daily routine which was perhaps typical for the elite gentlemen of his day: "At night after dinner he usually went out. At home he had given out that he went to see his friend Nawab Puttan, but he went to his mistress, Babban Jan, a young dancing girl. . . . Mir Nihal had rented a house for her. . . . She lived there and entertained him with her conversation and songs and her lithe figure and young body. He came back home at twelve or one and went to bed."[3]

Ahmed Ali succinctly describes the different classes of women involved in the oldest profession: "The prostitutes were of two kinds, the cultured ones and whores. The cultured ones were patronized by the rich and well-to-do. Young men were sent to them to learn manners and the art of polite conversation; and the older people came to enjoy their dancing, music, and their company in general" (p. 39). Mir Nahal and men of his standing patronized women of the cultured sort either occasionally or on a long-term basis. The segregated status of upper-class Muslim wives and daughters during this period, combined with the great wealth and leisure of their husbands and fathers, led almost inevitably to the formalization and acceptability of such liaisons. A wife was not expected to be well versed in the courtesan's arts; something would be amiss if she were. Rather, the two types of women performed different functions.

As Mir Nihal reflects on the approaching death of his mistress, he asks himself: "Who would care for him when she had gone? His wife was there, no doubt; and so were the children. But the world they lived in was a domestic world. There was no beauty in it and no love. Here, at Babban Jan's, he had built a quiet corner for himself where he could always retire and forget his sorrows" (p. 109). In a social system in which early arranged marriages were the rule and interaction between men and women was regulated strictly, relationships with courtesans provided men with opportunities for relaxation and entertainment that were not otherwise available.

In India today, of course, the market for courtesans has all but vanished. Political independence and socioeconomic progress have altered the class system drastically. The courtesan of Lucknow has gone the way of America's village smithy, a victim of role obsolescence. India's caste system makes it more difficult for the courtesan, however, because even if she trains herself for other employment, she is still marked by her family heritage. R. K. Narayan, perhaps India's best-known writer in English, deals with such a woman in *The Guide* *(1958)*. Rosie, who is the female protagonist, and her husband have employed as a tour guide one Raju, the narrator of the story. Rosie herself brings up the question of her own heritage in an early conversation with Raju:

> "Can you guess to what class I belong?" I looked her up and down and ventured, "The finest, whatever it may be, and I don't believe in class or caste. You are an honor to your caste, whatever it may be."
> "I belong to a family traditionally dedicated to the temples as dancers: my mother, grandmother, and, before her, her mother. Even as a young girl, I danced in our village temple. You know how our caste is viewed?"
> "It's the noblest caste on earth," I said.
> "We are viewed as public women," she said plainly. . . . "We are not considered respectable; we are not considered civilized."[4]

Rosie has obtained a master's degree in economics and has married a man with no relatives (and therefore no one to be horrified that his bride is by birth a dancing girl). She located her spouse through a newspaper advertisement for "an educated, good-looking girl to marry a rich bachelor of academic interests. *No caste* restrictions" (p. 74). She gives up dancing for her husband but later, because of extreme unhappiness and Raju's urging, takes it up again. Her husband refuses to have anything further to do with her, and the remainder of the novel focuses on the meteoric rise and equally precipitous decline of her dancing career as the famous Nalini, under the management of the impresario Raju. Significantly, Rosie, a married woman, is not virginal when she encounters Raju; the fact of her dancer's heritage implies that one should not expect her to follow the demure path of the Hindu wife.

If a dancer is assumed to be a courtesan, what of women who want to dance without taking on other implied aspects of the dancer's role? Given the dancer's dubious reputation, it is hardly surprising that the typical Indian husband would be aghast at the thought of his wife taking up that art as a form of recreation or employment. In *Andhere band kamre mẽ (Lingering Shadows)*, the contemporary Hindi novelist Mohan Rakesh deals with the problem of Nilima, a would-be dancer, and her husband, Harbans. Set in the 1950s, the novel describes the couple's troubled relationship as each of them relates it to their mutual friend, the novel's narrator. Harbans moves to London; Nilima stays in India to study dancing and to exert a sort of control over her husband. As she explains, "Let him go! I'll go south and learn *Bharata natyam....* Whatever Harbans may think, he can't live away from me. I know it only too well. Let him try."[5] She finally joins him in England, but then she wants to join a dance troupe and tour Europe. He forbids her to do so. She disobeys. The troupe returns to London minus Nilima and a Sikh drummer and a Burmese dancer. When Nilima eventually shows up, it is clear that she did not have an affair with either of those men, even though Harbans expects the worst.

Whereas R. K. Narayan's Rosie is a dancer by birth, Nilima is a proper wife and a dancer by training only; promiscuity in her case would be virtually unthinkable. She has taken up dancing as a sort of hobby, as others might take up

painting, golf, bridge, or volunteer work. While she attempts
to convince herself and others that her aspirations for a career
are legitimate, the attractions of home and family life ultimately override them.

South Asian writers depict prostitutes in terms radically
different from those which they use to describe courtesans.
The prostitute most frequently appears in works by "progressive" writers, i.e., those with social (and often socialist) concerns. Prostitution is employed in fiction to emphasize the
generally subjugated condition of Indian women and to assert
that a woman turns to the only economically feasible method
of survival in a time of great hardship. Several novelists have
written of women and girls who were forced into or to the
brink of prostitution during World War II or at the time of
independence and partition between India and Pakistan in
1947. Others have portrayed characters who find themselves
in this situation because of local, familial, or personal
hardships.

Bhabani Bhattacharya, a contemporary Bengali novelist,
has written two novels which deal with naive young country
girls in Calcutta during 1943. In *He Who Rides a Tiger*
(1955), Chandra Lekha, the motherless daughter of a black-
smith, is lured to the city by a female procurer for a whorehouse; she believes that the woman really is taking her to the
city's hospital to see her father, who allegedly has been injured
in an accident and is asking to see her. Once Chandra Lekha
discovers the ruse, she is trapped, without the money or wits
to engineer an escape. "She had spent the first two days in the
brothel in her room, with the door locked. . . . Today, her fifth
. . . the ogress spoke evil words to her all through the evening
and beat her with a whip. Finally, she took Lekha's clothes
away and gave her instead a thin blue sari. Nothing more. She
sprayed her with a heavy perfume."[6]

At this point, an unbelievable series of circumstances
brings Chandra Lekha's father to within earshot of the whore-

house, many miles from where either he or his daughter might be expected to be. Thinking he hears her voice but sure that it must be an illusion, he decides all the same that he must investigate; he bursts into her room in the nick of time and whisks her away to safety. Grasping at "every clue that increased his belief that he had not rescued Lekha too late" (p. 76), he is relieved to discover that her first and only customer had failed to have his way with her.

In *So Many Hungers* (1947), another of Bhattacharya's novels, the plight of the rural poor in 1943 is again a central topic. A village girl named Kajoli marries and soon becomes pregnant. In normal times, she and her husband and their relatives would have stayed on the land; but in 1943, many able-bodied men were in jail for refusing to cooperate with the British imperialist government, and still others were away at war. The Japanese seemed almost ready to attack India, having vanquished the Allied forces in their path. Harvests were small, and speculation in the grain market was rampant; people fled to the cities, especially Calcutta, in search of work and cash wages. Kajoli's husband, one of these would-be migrants, is shot to death by a guard as he tries to hop a train. As time passes and their situation becomes increasingly desperate, Kajoli and her brother and mother begin their own trek to the city in hopes of joining her husband, not knowing that he has died. Before their departure from the village, a woman comes to try to lure Kajoli into prostitution, tantalizing her with riches (rather than with fear for her father's safety, as with her counterpart in *He Who Rides a Tiger*). As the woman explains to Kajoli's mother:

> "Listen." Her small, keen eyes darted about and her voice was low, secretive.
> "She will live like a princess, your girl. . . . She will eat all her stomach can hold. She will have saris in dozens. . . ."
> As the meaning shaped slowly in her heart, very

slowly, the mother stood rigid, too dazed to speak a
word. . . .
    "There is a stream of money flowing these days. . . .
One good girl must learn a trick or two—I'll tell her what
she must know—and all will be well. . . ."
    The mother found her voice then. "Away with you,
woman," she shrieked. "Away with you, witch."[7]

Disaster is averted at this point, for Kajoli and her family
still have enough pride and energy to assert themselves. On
their way to Calcutta, Kajoli is raped by a soldier and loses the
child she is carrying. While the act—intercourse against her
will—is the same as that which the procurer was proposing, it
is significant that Kajoli was caught off her guard by an armed
man in the remote countryside rather than accosted by a
paying customer in a Calcutta brothel.
    Once in the city, the trio's situation becomes dire. Kajoli,
nevertheless, is able to avoid prostitution by engaging in exhibitionism instead:

A soldier moved from the group and dropped a rupee in
the begging bowl, which showed a few other silver coins.
    She said no word, only rose to her feet. . . . Her lips
curled with a smile that was somehow no smile. Then the
arms unfolded, stripping the ragged garment from her
breast. . . . Another rupee clinked into the bowl (pp.
192–93).

Finally Kajoli is forced to accept a procurer's offer of
eighty rupees for her virtue, or what remains of it. Her brother
is starving, and her mother is on the brink of death; eighty
rupees might purchase enough food to keep them alive for a
time. Kajoli reasons, "This body has been defiled on the high
road. Let it be defiled over and over again, then, if Mother's
life could be saved at that price." But, almost as with Chandra
Lekha, Kajoli is spared in the nick of time—by discovering
that she can earn a pittance by selling newspapers on commis-
sion. Even though her body is defiled, her baby lost through

miscarriage, and her virtue in a sense abandoned through exhibitionism, she always manages to avoid stooping to whoredom (p. 200).

Bhattacharya is not alone in allowing his heroines miraculous escapes from the clutches of lecherous men or avaricious procurers. Khushwant Singh, a noted Punjabi journalist and novelist, details the religious and cultural conflict that wrought havoc in northwest India in 1947 in his *Train to Pakistan* (1956). Hindus, Muslims, and Sikhs lived throughout the Punjab and surrounding areas before independence; however, with the advent of partition and the founding of Pakistan as a Muslim state, it became clear that Hindus no longer would be comfortable on the western side of the India – Pakistan border. Muslims, in turn, were moving to Pakistan in large numbers, either through their own preference or by force.

In *Train to Pakistan,* Singh deals primarily with the love of a village hooligan for a local girl. Although their romance obviously has a passionate, sexual aspect, we do not consider this woman (and she does not consider herself) to be promiscuous simply because she and her lover are not married. Indeed, as the novel ends, he sacrifices his life in order that she may live, an act which validates their commitment to each other, albeit outside the bonds of matrimony.

In the novel Singh also describes the pathetic situation of a young girl who has just been forced into prostitution. Although she goes through the motions of the courtesan's role, it is obvious from her first appearance that she has not been schooled in the art and that she and her companions are totally lacking in gentility: "The American car drove into the driveway. . . . Two men and two women stepped out. One of the men carried a harmonium and the other a pair of drums. One of the women was old, with white hair dyed a rich henna-orange. The other was a young girl whose mouth was bloated with betel leaf and who wore a diamond glistening on one side of her flat nose. . . . " She sings in a "shrill falsetto" which could not have been either pleasant or relaxing for her customer, Hukum Chand. But he obviously is interested in something other than music: "He stared at the girl. . . . She was only a child and not very pretty, just young and unexploited. . . . The thought that she was perhaps younger than his own daughter flashed across his mind. He drowned it quickly in another whisky. . . . When all was said and done she was a prostitute and looked it."

As with Bhattacharya's Chandra Lekha, this girl is snatched by a benevolent fate from the very arms of the lecher who would deflower her:

> She allowed herself to be dragged onto the table amongst the plates covered with stale meatballs and cigarette ash. . . . The girl suffered his pawing without protest. . . . Hukum Chand began fumbling with her dress.
>
> From [the village] came sounds of people shouting and the agitated barking of dogs. Hukum Chand looked up. Two shots rang out and silenced the barking and shouting. With a loud oath Hukum Chand left the girl. She got up, brushing and adjusting her sari. . . . [8]

The eruption of Hindu-Muslim strife has at least spared the honor of one young girl that evening.

Yashpal, a Hindi story writer and novelist of Marxist inclinations, has written vividly of middle- and lower-class women who find themselves in untenable situations. In "Ek sigret" ("One Cigarette"), the protagonist is turned out of her in-laws' house for possessing a single cigarette, a gift from her husband when he was last home on leave from the army. His parents gain the young man's ear, and he openly repudiates her when she seeks him out at his distant military cantonment. With no means of livelihood and nowhere to go (for no self-respecting Indian woman would ask to return to the home of her parents after they have seen to her marriage), she clearly will be forced to earn her living with her only marketable asset: her body. The story closes thus:

Manahar [the lecher who had been following her to the cantonment] waited patiently to see how the matter would end. Vajdatt acknowledged the fact that Damati was his wife, but when the court placed her in his care, he refused to accept her. . . . Hearing this, Damati gasped. . . .

The magistrate . . . rendered his decision: "You can go wherever you like now." The world grew dark before Damati's eyes, but she had to leave the courtroom. . . .

Manahar said comfortingly: "There was no reason to be angry [when he earlier tried to entrap her on the way to the cantonment]. I didn't mean to bother you. . . . Come. My house is yours."

Damati thought for a moment, then walked along with him. . . . Tears flowed from her eyes.[9]

Here, as elsewhere, pimps and procurers are portrayed as wicked, for they lead helpless or unsuspecting women into prostitution. On the other hand, madams may be evil (as in Bhattacharya's novels) or benign and cultivated, as in *The Courtesan of Lucknow* or in Manohar Malgonkar's *Bend in the Ganges*.[10] In the latter, it is significant that the house of ill fame is located in Lahore, a city (now in Pakistan) somewhat like Lucknow in its atmosphere of cultivation, even in the 1940s, when the novel takes place. Madams of the houses in both these works have beautiful, talented, and experienced girls staffing their establishments. The clients are wealthy and cultivated; none would dream of having his way with a woman in the midst of stale meatballs and cigarette butts, as described in *Train to Pakistan*.

Few Indian women novelists have portrayed prostitutes, although many have depicted women of different ages, status, and race who become involved with men, either extramaritally or premaritally. Sex for love and sex for money remain two completely different matters. In *Nectar in a Sieve*, her first published novel (1954), the well-known Indian English writer Kamala Markandaya joins Bhattacharya, Singh, Yashpal, and others who assert that prostitution is a last resort in times of extreme economic hardship.

Markandaya shows a teenage girl, Ira, taking to the streets of her village in a time of famine; her employment enables her to pay for the milk that keeps her youngest brother from starving. Ira's parents neither stand idly by nor encourage the activities of their daughter. Her mother, the novel's narrator, suspects but refuses to confront the real implications of her daughter's evening excursions: "'Where do you go?' I repeated. 'Tell me only where you go.' 'Do not ask,' she said. 'It is better that you should not know.'"[11] Ira's brother ultimately dies despite the milk, implying that prostitution is not a guarantee of long-term survival.

Ira was not a virgin when she took up prostitution. She had been married several years earlier but had been returned to her parental home by her husband when it became clear that she was not able to provide him with an heir. Thus, she fits the pattern seen in the other works analyzed so far: Women who have been married (Ira, Kajoli in So Many Hungers, and Damati in "One Cigarette") are vulnerable to present or future violations of their bodies, whereas those who begin as virgins (in He Who Rides a Tiger or Train to Pakistan) escape defloration by bizarre coincidence.

Although Ira was childless during her marriage, she becomes pregnant after she takes up prostitution. (Thus, we are led to believe that her husband might have been the cause of her childlessness, even though it was she who received the blame and bore the stigma.) Her child is born an albino, "marked," we assume, because of the circumstances of his conception. But he is the son for whom she has longed, and both she and her family accept him lovingly, even though he is a bastard and an albino. When a woman comes to call soon after the child's birth, Ira's brother defends the baby and, indirectly, his sister by saying, "It's only a question of getting used to. Who is to say this colour is right and that is not?" (pp. 122–23). Ultimately, the rest of the villagers grow to tolerate the child, for his mother's good motives (in providing food for her starving brother during a time of hardship and general famine) take the edge off her promiscuous behavior.

For prostitutes like Ira, money is the be-all and end-all. No pretense of aesthetic taste or talent is maintained by a solitary woman who lurks in a darkened doorway, ready to pick up the first customer who happens her way. While those who work for madams or pimps sometimes attempt to dazzle their partners with gauze and glittering finery, a prostitute cannot learn in a few days or years what a courtesan has assimilated and practiced over the course of a lifetime. Whereas sex rarely is detailed with regard to the courtesan, it often is described or at least implied in fictional passages dealing with prostitutes and is almost always handled in a lurid manner.

As the above examples have shown, the images of the courtesan and the prostitute, while by no means new or uncommon in Indian literature, are far from identical. The distinct status and role of each character type is socially defined and carefully delineated. Works which describe courtesans must nowadays be of a historical nature, given the demise of that profession. (Who can afford to live today in the style of the princes of old?) On the other hand, wars, religious conflicts, and famines can bring about grave peril for millions within a matter of days or weeks. Modernization and urbanization also have their effects on society, even though they act more slowly; people are displaced from their land or from their hereditary occupations by urban sprawl or by the advent of new technologies. Although women of certain classes and in certain fields have made great strides and have achieved worldwide visibility, the great masses of Indian women remain poor, uneducated, and unprepared (both psychologically and operationally) to support themselves. For these and myriad other reasons, it is quite unlikely that prostitution will disappear from the South Asian subcontinent or that South Asian writers will cease to portray it in their literary works.

The Fate of the Fallen Woman in *Maggie* and *Sister Carrie*

LAWRENCE E. HUSSMAN, JR.

THE TWO MOST FAMOUS turn-of-the-century representations of the fallen woman in American literature appear in Stephen Crane's *Maggie: A Girl of the Streets* and Theodore Dreiser's *Sister Carrie*. Each has long been recognized as a work of historical importance in the struggle for a realistic fiction that would deal forthrightly with previously taboo subject matter. Crane's heroine is a girl driven by the poverty of her background into a career as a prostitute, while Dreiser's is a kept woman whose liaisons help her toward a career as a celebrated Broadway actress.

Despite our tendency to think of *Maggie* and *Sister Carrie* as revolutionary works which shocked the readers of their time, neither reached a significant audience until some years after their authors offered them to the public. Crane's sense that his story would offend the sensibilities of the reading public led him to secure its private circulation. Dreiser's novel, though accepted for publication, was distributed sparsely because of Frank Doubleday's second thoughts about its questionable situations. Had both works been normally published and enthusiastically launched, however, their respective receptions by the wider public might have been quite different.

Although three-quarters of a century of intervening criticism has conditioned modern readers to accept the myth that both novels were equally revolutionary, nothing could be further from the truth. *Sister Carrie* was genuinely subversive of the sexual standards for women of the time, but such a statement cannot be made concerning *Maggie.*

The reason that *Sister Carrie* was in fact a revolutionary work while *Maggie* was not can be found in the opposite ways in which Dreiser and Crane employed certain fictional formulae while discarding others and also in the two writers' different backgrounds. *Maggie* breaks new American ground in its subject matter: the filth and degradation of the slums, the socially destructive effects of alcoholism, the demimonde of the hooker. The novella appears to be a bold new step toward the liberation of American literature because of the relatively realistic veneer that Crane applies to its seamy surfaces.

Although Crane incongruously began the book while a fraternity man at Syracuse University, he did research his subject in some depth. While still in Syracuse, for example, he investigated the red-light district and interviewed some of its prostitutes. When he arrived in New York a few months later, he began roaming the Bowery, testing the characters and situations in the most recent draft of his story against reality. He became a dedicated observer of the denizens of the down-and-out district, resolving to make his study "sincere," a quality he judged to be missing from earlier nonfictional accounts which had not begun to suggest the horror of the squalid conditions, the brutality, or the tragedy of the wasted lives.

He set about gathering impressions in the manner of the notebook naturalist, sleeping in shelters with derelicts, standing in blizzard-buffeted bread lines, absorbing the dialect. But this was synthetic experience, not preordained by circumstances. Unlike Dreiser, Crane came from a background that was genteel though far from affluent. Crane's father was a respected Methodist minister, and his influence on his son can be observed in the moral assumptions that color the novelist's judgments in *Maggie*. Although Crane rejected the romantic settings and situations in the fiction of his time, he had no quarrel with the formulae that placed beautiful young women on pedestals, rued the effects of demon rum, or, finally and fatally for the novella, punished women who dared to use their bodies to survive the maelstrom of the city.

Maggie opens with a graphic scene designed to make the reader see the reality of Bowery life: gangs bent on establishing one of their own as king of the mountain, in this case a "heap of gravel."[1] Among the urchins, we meet Maggie's brother Jimmie, an aspiring tough who already has developed the "chronic sneer of ideal manhood," the badge of Bowery courage which is validated when he falls to fighting with the members of his own gang near the end of the scene. After Jimmie is dragged home by his father, Crane introduces a description of uncompromising domestic violence behind the "gruesome doorway" of the Johnsons' house. After Jimmie hits Maggie for suggesting that he fights too much, he is pummeled by his mother, both parents engage in a "lurid altercation," and the father, annoyed by the intoxicated condition of his wife, leaves the house bent on a "vengeful drunk" (pp. 8–9).

Thus, the hopelessly sordid conditions of slum life are set forth, and the reader is led to expect an unrelentingly tough-minded presentation. Indeed, the naturalistic literary mode which Crane chooses in the novella demands a high degree of verisimilitude. But when Crane turns his attention to Maggie, his realistic treatment of the material short-circuits. Instead of establishing his heroine's typicality as molded by her environment—a necessary quality in "case study" fiction—he stresses romantic qualities which set her apart not only from the street crowds but from her family as well. First, we are informed that the girl "blossomed in a mud puddle" to become that "most rare and wonderful production of a tenement district, a pretty girl" (p. 16). There is no inherent reason for Maggie to be pretty, though the argument has sometimes been made that Crane made her so in order to make believable her transformation into a prostitute at the end of the story. One stroll through a Bowery red-light district, however, should have been enough to disabuse Crane of the idea that it would have been necessary for his heroine to possess physical beauty to function there.

Maggie's attractiveness might signal to an attentive reader that Crane was not immune to the familiar slips twixt the typical naturalist's credo of objectivity and his practice in fiction. Without frequent visits from a turn-of-the-century version of the Bowery Avon lady, Maggie surely would not have stood out from her peers. Moreover, Crane makes the case that she is a girl of heightened sensitivity, though he in no way explains the source of her finer feeling. We are told that even as a child, she was disgusted by dirt while fighting with street gamins. But nowhere in the novella is there a positive role model for Maggie. Her mother is a drunken slattern whose characterization is uniformly negative. All around are violence and despair. Yet Maggie grows to a womanhood of tenderness as well as beauty, one of the least likely candidates in the Bowery to end up as a prostitute.

Crane's careless attitude toward detail further weakens credibility. In some instances, specifics which could help set the scene or establish character motivation are missing. In other cases, the details do not ring true. An example of missing detail occurs when Maggie is told by her brother that the time has come to "go on d'toif or go t'work." She opts for work in a collar and cuff factory. But the whole of her experience on the job is dispensed with in half a paragraph. Crane misses the opportunity to describe in detail the brutalizing labor which Bowery residents endured in the sweatshops if they were lucky enough to be employed. In so ignoring work-

ing conditions, he fails to provide Maggie with credible motivation for becoming a prostitute later. The reader may
legitimately ask why Maggie feels the need to take to the
streets when her factory job or another like it would seem to
be available. But literary historians point out that Crane
showed little interest in working conditions, an error of omis-
sion which probably would not have been committed by a
writer whose background included the necessity of demeaning
work.

When Maggie meets Pete, the flashy bartender who is to
become the agent of her moral destruction, her maidenly
behavior would do justice to the purest formula heroine of
romance. Again, the source of this finer feeling is mysterious.
She not only idealizes Pete beyond recognition, she even refuses him a kiss on their first date, a visit to a stage show.
Crane evidently felt that Maggie's Bowery dialect would suffice to make the scene believable.

But the snake is coiled in the garden during this first
encounter between the two. Pete is drinking beer during the
show, the initial indication that Crane is about to turn the
novella into a virtual sermon on the evils of demon rum and
related pleasures. Once Pete has succeeded in introducing
Maggie to sex, an acquaintanceship which has been curiously
denied her to this point in the novel, the path to prostitution is
paved. In a series of barroom scenes we see Maggie being led
into a variety of evils, including drinking. In one bar, for
example, a ballad singer-dancer performs each of her numbers
in "less gown." With heavy-handed foreshadowing, Pete and
Maggie encounter two "painted women" as they leave the bar
(pp. 38–39).

Crane's moralistic attitude is unmistakable in such
scenes, as he drops nearly all pretense of naturalistic objectivity. We need only recall that his father, Dr. Jonathan Town-
ley Crane, was the author of several temperance tracts
including *The Arts of Intoxication* (1870) and a book which

explored the dangers of other diversions (including novel reading) called *Popular Amusements* (1869). Stephen Crane took to self-conscious indulgence in familiar vices as part of an effort to exorcise his moral training, but his attempts were not entirely successful. His contemporaries noted, for instance, that often after ordering a drink with much bravado, he would leave it unconsumed the whole evening. He was also known to self-consciously light cigarettes only to let them burn down. Amy Lowell was on target when she said of Crane's rejected religion: "He disbelieved it and hated it, but he could not free himself from it."[2] We tend to remember the fact that Crane was forced to seek private publication for *Maggie* because of its incendiary subject, but we are prone to forget that the private publisher he induced to print the book was B.O. Flower, a crusading reform editor.

Once Maggie is rejected by her hypocritical parents and by Pete, who fears the wrath of the suddenly priggish Jimmie, the girl is forced into the streets, where her aimless wandering elicits the attention of men with "calculating eyes." Frightened by their appraising stares, she adopts "a demeanor of intentness" until she happens upon a stout gentleman with a kindly face. In perhaps the most famous vignette in the novella, the man makes a "convulsive movement" and takes a "vigorous side step" to save his respectability rather than save the "soul" before him (pp. 50–51). The stout gentleman rejects Maggie's implicit appeal for help, a rebuff that signals her descent into the red-light district.

The next scene, played out "several months" later, focuses on Maggie as an unaccountably successless whore, turned down serially by five prospective customers. Crane explains neither why a girl of Maggie's apparent moral resources is on the streets as opposed to the collar and cuff factory nor why a girl of Maggie's physical attributes is such a failure at her adopted profession. Furthermore, the melodramatic climax seriously compromises the novella's realistic intent. Rejected by her potential clientele, Maggie the reluctant lady of the evening welcomes the embrace of the river. No statistics exist concerning the percentage of prostitutes who committed suicide in New York during the 1890s, but the Aristotelian probability is that the percentage was quite small.

When Crane sent Maggie to her self-imposed doom, it was not only because of the logic of such a denouement given the characterization of his heroine as a girl of exceptional sensitivity but also because he was indulging his moral prejudices instead of breaking new ground with a realistic presentation of the prostitute's plight. *Maggie: A Girl of the Streets* is far from a revolutionary naturalistic document in its treatment of the woman's code of sexual conduct. Indeed, it moves only a quarter step forward, replacing death before dishonor with death immediately after dishonor. Crane had never been to war when he reconstructed the experiences and feelings of a soldier in *The Red Badge of Courage*. But whereas intuition and imagination served him well in that justly praised novel, such was not the case in *Maggie*. That work is seriously flawed because it was impossible for him to intuit and imagine the thought processes of a prostitute.

Sister Carrie is, from the outset, the story of a woman who is not above using her sexuality to get ahead. The novel's opening scene establishes for Dreiser's heroine the possibility that her body might be a medium of exchange when the traveling salesman, Drouet, offers her twenty dollars after meeting her on a train. Although, because of the temper of the times, this potentially explosive material is handled subtly, the point of the tendered bargain is inescapable when Carrie goes to live with Drouet a bit later in the novel. The immediate result was to provide the kind of motivation so strikingly absent in Crane's heroine. Carrie arrives in Chicago from a small Wisconsin town and is overwhelmed by the possibilities for pleasure, position, and power which the great metropolis in the making represents. Chicago is compared to a seducer whispering an irresistible falsehood which "relaxes, then weakens, then perverts the simpler human perceptions" (p. 2).[3]

Much of Dreiser's youth had been spent in extravagant longing for the same commodities that stimulate Carrie's dreams. That he associated these things with Chicago is illustrated clearly in the many retrospective rhapsodies dedicated to the city in his autobiographical writings. Since Dreiser invests Carrie not only with the urgent need for personal fulfillment which Chicago incited in him but also with "an average little conscience," her habitual capitulation to temptation is justified psychologically.

She is only temporarily able to resist Drouet's implicit offer to make her a "dishonest woman." At this point, Dreiser's knowledge of the pressures of poverty and the respect for detail which his long journalistic apprenticeship provided him help make Carrie's transformation from innocent to kept woman believable. She moves into a dismal flat with her sister and brother-in-law. The constricted horizons of this working-class milieu in no way mesh with Carrie's dreams. Here the simplest pleasures are regarded as wasteful. In order to make her own way toward the financial security which alone can make possible the life she longs for, she takes to the streets in search of a job. Dreiser provides a great many convincing details from his own experience about the search as well as the job. The reader walks the streets with Carrie, gauging the reactions of office managers, enduring serial humiliations, making with her "that wearisome, baffled retreat which the seeker for employment at nightfall too often makes" (p. 29). Once Carrie finds a job in a shoe factory, we experience with her the distasteful routine and the nightly fatigue which outweigh her monetary rewards. The details which Dreiser provides are quite realistic, down to the description of Carrie as a "very average looking shop girl with the exception of her features," which were "slightly more even than common" (p. 37). No "blossom in a mud puddle" she.

When the opportunity to become Drouet's mistress for profit again presents itself, Carrie is quick to assent. For a time, the role of the salesman's kept woman satisfies her, since it allows her to build up her wardrobe and provides her with an entry to Chicago's restaurants and theaters. But Drouet's neglect and her burgeoning ambition to become an actress lead to her interest in the stylish bar manager, Hurstwood. When he spirits her off to Montreal and New York with the help of a ruse, her resistance is feeble because she believes that he can help her realize her theatrical ambitions and because she has already known the life of a kept woman. She comes to accept her liaison with Hurstwood, but when he loses his job after three years, he disintegrates quickly, and Carrie's compassion for him is limited indeed. By the time he has come to the brink of suicide, Carrie has established herself as a celebrated Broadway actress and is cultivating a relationship with yet another man.

Despite the formulaic nature of Carrie's success story, which transforms her from small-town innocent to Broadway starlet, the conclusion of Dreiser's novel is infinitely more revolutionary than that of *Maggie: A Girl of the Streets*. Although Carrie has defied established morality by living with two men and has abandoned her prescribed sex role by giving to each anything but subservient devotion, her only punishment is a vague feeling that she has not yet found total fulfillment—the common lot of modern man and woman. Luck and her opportunistic sexual alliances have provided her with gowns, carriages, applause, and power. *Sister Carrie* shows that the transgressions by which we define a fallen woman may in fact lead to a fortunate fall. Carrie becomes a wiser and more sophisticated person in part by virtue of her "vices." No wonder Frank Doubleday had second thoughts about publishing the novel and tried everything he could to avoid distributing it.

Dreiser's first extended work of fiction is considerably

more advanced than Crane's. *Maggie: A Girl of the Streets* achieved an important place in American literary history through its treatment of the touchy subject of prostitution and its forthright portrayal of Bowery conditions. But as a psychological profile of a prostitute, it is seriously flawed and vastly overrated. Crane strove diligently to capture in fiction the life of the downtrodden. But in creating character and situation, he was forced to rely on observation as opposed to introspection and direct experience. That Crane was merely slumming in *Maggie* soon becomes obvious. *Sister Carrie,* on the other hand, successfully explores the emotions of a woman who knows the agony of deprivation and knows that she must do anything to escape it, including using sexual favors for advancement.

Dreiser was sometimes guilty of abandoning his advantage of firsthand experience, as in the sentimental and implausible *Jennie Gerhardt.* And when Crane wrote from personal experience, he was capable of a most impressive verisimilitude, such as that which informs "The Open Boat." But in their first extended works, both of which deal with the theme of the fallen woman, Dreiser was much the more true to life and therefore by far the more dangerous to those who held inviolable the sexual standards of the time for women.

The Uncommon Prostitute:
The Contemporary Image in an
American Age of Pornography

JAMES M. HUGHES

> Be composed—be at ease with me—I am Walt Whitman,
> liberal and lusty as Nature,
> Not till the sun excludes you do I exclude you,
> Not till the waters refuse to glisten for you and the leaves
> to rustle for you, do my words refuse to glisten and
> rustle for you.
> My girl I appoint with you an appointment, and I charge
> you that you make preparation to be worthy to meet
> me,
> And I charge you that you be patient and perfect till I
> come.
> Till then I salute you with a significant look that you do
> not forget me.
>
> WALT WHITMAN, 1860

> *Prostitute* A person, usually a woman, who engages in
> sexual intercourse for money. . . .
>
> *Random House Dictionary, 1968*

> Ratso . . . claimed that prostitution had always been the
> hardest profession in the world as well as the most
> competitive—and even worse in today's world, where
> the commodity was being given away free in such lib-

eral quantities. The only way to do really well at it was
to rob the patron, but this required an adroitness and a
sense of timing Ratso felt was lacking in his cowboy
friend, and he did not encourage him to enter this extension of the market.

JAMES LEO HERLIHY, 1965

THE CONTEMPORARY AMERICAN WRITER includes
the uncommon prostitute among his or her diverse characterizations. Newly liberalized standards of taste and decorum
make Walt Whitman's 1860 declaration "To a Common Prostitute" seem quaint, sexist, moralistic, condescending, and,
ironically, dirty. "And I charge you that you be patient and
perfect till I come" not only seems today a play on role
reversal—who charges whom—but a male fantasy of the perfect female partner who must be "patient and perfect" until *he*
reaches climax.

Indeed, when innuendo and double entendre themselves,
however unintended they may have been, seem quaint, when
sexual activities are freely admitted and described, it must be a
very uncommon kind of prostitute who will get the attention
of readers. The narrative demands of fiction for heroines and
heroes are traditional explanations for contemporary variations on the theme of the prostitute with the heart of gold, a
theme that nicely combines elements of materialism and sentimentality. Sentimentality persists, but with a new emphasis on
frankness of expression and with a decrease in judgmental
moralism. The supposedly uncommon male prostitute receives
newly emphasized attention. But it is in the autobiography of
famous prostitutes that the uncommonness of today's literary
prostitute becomes most clear. Like others emerging from
closets and sculleries, today's prostitutes are publicly demand-
ing rights, including the literary right to tell their stories.
Thus, the new sexual freedoms that may make prostitution

more hard-pressed competitively also put a premium on the publicity of special, uncommon skills. Literary emphases on the exceptional, however realistically expressed, coincide with new public tolerance, awareness, and interest. The contemporary literary prostitute is indeed worthy to meet the public eye, not to mention Whitman's transcendentally more discerning one.

EXOTIC HEART OF GOLD:
THE TRADITIONAL SENTIMENTALITY

British writer Richard Mason's *The World of Suzie Wong*[1] popularized the traditional image of a redeemable prostitute, the painter's model who leaves a Hong Kong brothel, tuberculosis, and a dead illegitimate child all behind to enter British society. The Asiatic and British connections underline the popular appeal in America: Safely exotic fallen women cannot rise much farther than Anglo-Saxon society.

Mason's novel and popular American stage and screen adaptations end with Suzie Wong maintaining only her realism, her professional nose for phoniness; she has left her profession itself behind. This conclusion is characterized by touch-and-go melodrama: Will Suzie Wong be redeemed? At one point, the narrator-husband laments her apparent promiscuity: "I wondered vaguely why she had done it; I suppose it was just a reversion to type. You couldn't keep a good whore down. Or at least up." This classical British putdown is accepted by colonial Suzie herself: "I told you I was no good. I told you I would just give you trouble" (p. 316).

But it is precisely Suzie's knowledge of herself and her acceptance of her husband's British standards that allow her, quite uncommonly, to save the hero himself from his own hypocrisy. Suzie sees through her husband's infatuation with his success as a painter (not so incidentally of brothel scenes) and emphasizes not the social success (experience from which whores and ex-whores are usually exempt) but the work (experience that whores and ex-whores know very well). The novel thus finally concludes with a revealing bit of dialogue in which Suzie tells her husband:

> "I like you today. I like you when you work, and wear that dirty old coat full of paint."
> "And when don't you like me?"
> "When you get stuck-up and talk too much" (p. 338).

This saving of Suzie Wong extends, at least temporarily, to her effect on her former fellow workers when she returns to her Hong Kong place of work. The pat happy ending barely hides a moral: "And I do not think there has been another night like it at the Nam Kab before or since. The girls were far too excited by Suzie's return to think of working" (p. 340).

The World of Suzie Wong popularized the image of a good girl who happens to be a prostitute. It is modern only to the extent that this happenstance is judged only indirectly; it is essential to the plot that Suzie be both prostitute and saved, that her past experience contribute positively to her new life. The world Suzie escapes at least gives her saving knowledge of other worlds.

Suzie was the star of the world she left behind. Few modern literary prostitutes, male or female, will be considered otherwise than stars. Social hierarchy within the subculture is the link between the British "classy" stereotype of Suzie Wong and more liberated American types.

MADAMS: THE HOOKER ELITE

In 1953, in her autobiography, *A House Is Not a Home*,[2] Polly Adler boasted, "in July of 1939 . . . I, Polly Adler, was written about in *Fortune*" (p. 333). *Fortune* was interested in her business acumen; it might well have echoed her own assessment of her economic role: "I had a very definite place in the social structure. I belonged, I had a job to do, and I could find satisfaction in doing it the very best way I knew how" (p. 318).

Nineteen years later, Xaviera Hollander, in her "own story," *The Happy Hooker*,[3] will echo Polly Adler, calling herself a "woman of class, happy in her profession, and basically doing a necessary service" (p. 5). Hollander is not displeased to hear herself described as "New York's most notorious madam" (p. 4). Similarly, Polly Adler boasted "New York's most famous bordello" (p. 4).

Each uncommonly successful prostitute stresses an aspect of business goodwill. In 1953, Adler declared: "My patrons were not just ambulatory bankrolls, but individual human beings," and she treated each as if he were "an honored guest" (p. 319). Hollander echoed many businesspeople when, in 1972, she claimed: "It hasn't been strictly commerce, I *have* tried to give some happiness to those men, even though they paid for it" (p. 309). Each autobiography details the development of this profitable goodwill despite harassment by both criminals and police.

It is her precarious position between law and crime which gives the successful madam her heroic stature. Hollander notes her "aggressive leadership, a head for figures, and a matchless stamina" as qualities allowing her to attain the goal of "star in this business" (pp. 147–48). Adler, realistically appraising the difficulties in the way of going into legitimate business, accepts her fate as a starting point for even greater success: "I couldn't live my reputation down—all right then, I'd live up to it" (p. 283). Adler and Hollander are, then, uncommonly folk or pop heroines, examples of independent women who rise on their own merits.

The significant difference between Adler and Hollander is more a matter of style than of substance. Adler is discreet about both the mechanics of sex and her own sexuality. She boasts of her "reputation for running a clean house . . . at no time would I allow off-color conversation or the practice of unnatural sex by any of my girls" (p. 93). By contrast, Hollander is explicit in all respects: "I happen to like to fuck" (p. 41). Her "house of pleasure" (p. 176) caters to all tastes short of actual violence: "I refuse to do anything that might cause anyone real damage" (p. 226). Otherwise she is prepared.

Hollander has her bottle of mouthwash to counteract the distasteful sperm that she is prepared to swallow (p. 134). Her book reflects the age of pornography's popular interest in what another age would have called prurient detail. But both Adler and Hollander admit their illegal professionalism openly, secure in their unusual success. Both explain their survival despite the threats of all too orderly criminal elements and all too disorderly police elements. Detective fiction extends the image of the prostitute working for justice outside the law. Successful madam and succesful girl detective both owe their force as literary characters to the ambiguity of law and order in an age of pornography.

PROSTITUTE DETECTIVE

The legacy of hard-boiled detective fiction, the essentially ambiguous morality of the modern city, can be very useful in an age of pornography. The skeptical realism of the prostitute becomes a commonly uncommon perspective through which the hypocritical laws and destructive criminal orders of society may be seen. Prostitution's traditional literary legacy of a heart of gold is the sentimental justification for the heroine's uncommon devotion to justice. Although she may be forced by circumstances around her to become a decoy for danger, the prostitute as detective at least chooses to make the best of the challenge of those circumstances. In the detective novel, streetwalker or call girl can call herself madam in at least one scene.

Tony Kenrick's *The Chicago Girl*[4] (1976) is the story of lost jewels. A gangster died before he was able to give stolen jewels to his prostitute girl friend. The gangster's loyal henchman seeks the girl and has a false claimant killed. The book's hero, significantly a crime journalist and not a detective, attempts to find a prostitute who can impersonate the gangster's missing girl friend. His primary motives are the insurance reward and a good news story. It is the uncommon nature of the missing prostitute which provides the difficulty: She is upper-class British, and her impersonator must be able to slip into the accent of her origin under pressure. The first part of the novel follows the pattern of Shaw's *Pygmalion*. Wanda Podenda, a.k.a. Marsha Williams, must learn to act an upper-class role:

> "You ever done any acting?"
> "Sweetie, I go on every night" (p. 16).

Nevertheless, the risk is too great, the time too short. The second part of the novel reverses the Pygmalion theme: Amateur British actress Jenny Copland must be coached by Wanda/Marsha to pretend to be the real prostitute hiding her really upper-class British identity.

Further explanation of the plot not only would violate the rule against giving away a mystery's solution but would be to no purpose. The significance of the image of the prostitute in *The Chicago Girl* is the emphasis on acting and pretense. Xaviera Hollander emphasized theatricality, especially in freak scenes, which had to be as "well-staged [as] one-act plays," requiring "the patience of Job and the psychology of a Freud" (p. 209–10). The con in *The Chicago Girl* is so well staged that neither its director nor the reader is sure that it is a con; Jenny Copland's performance is so convincing that all seem confused. The convincing confusion of illusion and reality reminds one of Polly Adler's dictum: "No woman is born a whore and any woman may become one" (p. 104).

The real prostitute in *The Chicago Girl,* the acting coach, gets beaten up by her pimp. The detective story ends with the hero lamenting her fate and at the same time setting the reader up for the sentimentally moral redemption:

> "I feel bad about her," he said. "I dragged her in and she's got nothing to show but scars."
> "That's not quite true. She's quitting the Life"
> (p. 190).

Brian De Palma's film and book *Dressed to Kill*[5] expands the themes of fantasy, theatricality, and double identity. The book begins with transvestite schizophrenic Bobbi at one of the institutions that may in an age of permissiveness compete with prostitution: "They had come here to try to score. To score, she thought. A sporting metaphor. The game of fucking. The gladiatorial arena of a single's bar" (p. 3). The story's killer is at once murderer and victim, patient and psychiatrist. The role of psychiatrist in *Dressed to Kill* itself suggests prostitution, and one can recall Xaviera Hollander's defense of her therapy: "My method? Basically the same principle as Masters and Johnson, only they charge thousands and it's called therapy. I charge $50 and it's called prostitution" (p. 170).

Dressed to Kill consistently calls attention to the ambiguity of names, callings, and roles. In the book, the wife, Kate, describes sex with her husband with words that seem familiar in countless scenes of prostitution:

> "He climbs on, climbs off, as if I was a blowup doll you could order from Frederick's mail-order catalogue."
> *(I'm Kate, five foot three, and I'm built to please.)*
> "I should get an Oscar," she thought. "I'm expert at making him think he's good" (p. 11).

Polly Adler could comment here: "To ninety-nine out of a hundred girls going to bed with a customer is a joyless, even distasteful, experience" (p. 127). Yet the experienced prostitute knows how to "give a man his money's worth" (p. 337).

Some wives may be just as good actresses and may be playing a role not unlike the one played by the prostitute.

But the central character in *Dressed to Kill* is Liz, a call girl. She witnesses the murder and chooses to become the decoy to catch the killer in order to prove her own innocence. Liz has the commercial instincts already noted by Adler and Hollander: "She had given herself two years to get in and out of this game. Invest and save, save and invest, and don't squander a single opportunity" (p. 31). But her instinctive heart of gold does indeed involve her in a crime which threatens to squander more than her savings. Her involvement is central; she is positioned between the law and the murderer. The law accuses her of guilt: "You're a hooker, Liz. A pretty expensive hooker, but a hooker just the same, and right now everything points in your direction, doesn't it?" (p. 58). Liz knows that the murderer saw her:

> "*I saw the killer.*
> *Nobody else*" (p. 62).

The conclusion confronts an uncommonly heroic hooker detective pretending to be a patient with a woman-patient killer pretending (?) to be a man-psychiatrist. The dialog between them highlights the special role of prostitute in an age of pornography, the role of professional expert at what for others is mostly amateur.

> "Believe me, it's bad. And I'm an expert on bad."
> "What makes you an expert on bad?"
> "I should tell you up front—I'm a hooker. You name it, I've done it."
> He was silent for a moment. Then, "You enjoy what you do?"
> "Yeah. Sometimes. I like the idea that I can turn a guy on."
> "Do you ever have sex where there's no money involved?" he asked.
> "Do you give free consultations?" (p. 166).

The world has forced Liz into prostitution; "the world was a hard place without bread and . . . the most saleable commodity you possessed was your body" (p. 52). Circumstances also force Liz into detection to save herself: *"your only weapon, kid, is your body"* (p. 167). Liz's uncommonness resides in her heroic follow-through on the consequences of her instinctive (she reached out to try to save the dying victim) and economic determinants. Such heroism usually is reserved for men. Is there any to be found in that now more commonly described world of the uncommonly male prostitute, the hustler?

HUSTLERS, COWBOYS, AND GIGOLOS

The heroism of the male prostitute is undercut by the clinical approach to this relatively uncommon literary type. All literature detailing the life of a subculture may have to inform its readers in a self-conscious way; in the age of the case study, this informational aspect is stressed. Some hardcore pornography is itself clinical in its mechanical objectivity, its sense of seeing another kind of life form through a conveniently one-way glass.

Thus, the hero of John Rechy's *City of Night*[6] (1963) gives, albeit in oversimplistic Freudian terms, an explanation for his hustling:

> When I was almost eight years old, my father taught me this: He would say to me: "Give me a thousand," and I knew this meant I should hop on his lap and then he would fondle me—intimately—and he'd give me a penny, sometimes a nickel. At times when his friends—old grey men—came to our house, they would ask for "a thousand." And I would jump on their laps too. And I would get nickel after nickel, going around the table.
>
> And later, a gift from my father would become a token of a truce from the soon-to-blaze hatred between us (p. 14).

Polly Adler and Xaviera Hollander are not alone, then, in answering the traditional question: "What is a nice girl like you doing in a place like this?" Polly Adler's book is her answer: "During the twenty-five years I ran a house, it seemed to me that my time was about equally divided between answering questions and avoiding answering them" (p. 4). The answers confront condemnation head on: "Patrons who would despise me for being a madam . . . because I was associated with the side of their own nature of which they were most ashamed" (p. 286).

The dilemma of the male hustler is his own fear of identification with his sense of shame. Rechy's hero quotes another hustler's refusal to identify male hustling with homosexuality: "'It bugged me, him thinking I was queer or something. I told him fuck off. I wasn't gonna make it for free'" (p. 40). Each male hustler plays many roles, but he must not be gay:

> Youngmanout of a jobbut looking; dontgiveadamnyoung-man drifting; perennial hustler easytomakeout; young-manlostinthebigcity pleasehelpmesir . . . the stance, the jivetalk—a mixture of jazz, joint, junk sounds—the almost disdainful, disinterested, but at the same time, inviting look; the casual way of dress . . . you had to play it almost-illiterate (p. 32).

Adler and Hollander both suggest homosexuality's place as a refuge for many female prostitutes; for the male hustler, homosexuality is as much a doom as old age.

Rechy's hero has his first meaningful, and the book's first explicit, sex with a man named Jeremy in New Orleans. Jeremy asks the question that the hero has been avoiding: "I'm sure youve thought you have a definite advantage of whatever kind over the people youve been with, because theyve wanted *you*, because theyve paid *you*—some sort of victory beyond the sex-experience, beyond the money. (But dont you need them just as badly?)" (p. 355). Rechy's hero rejects the answer implicit in Jeremy's question.

So does Joe Buck in James Leo Herlihy's *Midnight Cowboy*[7] (1965). Joe, the costumed cowboy determined to sell himself to the women of New York, discovers the truth of one of the legends of Rechy's male hustler world. Again it is Jeremy who asks the question:

> "Wouldn't your masculinity be compromised much less if you tested your being 'wanted' with women instead of men?"
> "It's easier to hustle men" (p. 350).

Discovering the truth and accepting it are two different stories. Joe Buck cannot accept himself in the role that he is forced to adopt. The climax of *Midnight Cowboy* is the violent role reversal occasioned by Joe's need to get money in order to get Rizzo to Florida:

> Joe picked up the table lamp and held it high in the air. "You want to give me fifty dollars? Or you want your head broke open?"
> The expression on Locke's face made his preference perfectly clear: He looked with longing at the lamp, and his body remained pressed against the table.
> Realizing what was being required of him, Joe began to feel sick. It began to seem that the positions were reversed, as if Locke held the weapon (p. 175).

Joe Buck's lack of heroic stature is here revealed; he rationalizes the violence that he inflicts and continues to see himself only in the role of victim.

The hero of Timothy Harris's *American Gigolo*[8] is less than the movie role would seem to demand to serve as effective showcase for Richard Gere, a new male sex symbol. The romantic possibilities are suggested by scenes in which the gigolo goes about his business with uncommon success, the kind of success only fantasized by Joe Buck.

"Who are you?" she demanded in a whisper.
"Well, I . . . ah . . . do this for a living."
"Do what?"
"I pick up women."
She stared at me in perfect bewilderment.
"They pay me. It's what I do" (pp. 14–15).

Such dialog comes right from Paul Schrader's screenplay and celebrates with rare verve the possibilities of male prostitution in the straight world.

Unfortunately, the fashion for introspection and the penchant for clinical details confuse the romantic image in the novel form of the story. The novel, unlike the film, finds it necessary to explain the gigolo's physiological secret, the male prostitute's possible disadvantage. The hero is able to perform when, in his own words, "I find some feature or aspect in the woman which gives me a feeling of melancholy and that generally leads to arousal" (p. 18). Lest this stimulus be mistaken for a sense of compassion, the hero is even more explanatory: "I need this sense of their humanity and their suffering in order to desire them" (p. 19). The gigolo succeeds only to the extent that he can feel superior.

In any case, the male prostitute in a straight world remains less heroic a figure than his female counterpart. The lingering sexism of the age of pornography and the rampant sexism of pornography itself may account for this discrepancy. In the marketplace, men would prefer to see themselves as buyers, and the men who sell themselves in that same marketplace are condemned to fear for their own masculinity. In Rechy's novel, Jeremy suggests, of course, that buyer and seller may be one and the same: "There isnt any difference, really between the hunter and the hunted. The hunted makes himself available—usually passively, but available, nevertheless. Thats his way of hunting" (p. 358). And that passivity is, ironically for the he-man male hustler, an attribute of the female stereotype. It is, furthermore, a passivity not neces-

sarily familiar in view of the number of aggressively successful
if not heroic female prostitutes in the literature.

INNOVATIONS AND UNCOMMON STYLES

Sometimes the writer may be the real hero. The writer
may dare traditional styles and develop new expressions of
traditional stereotypes. In 1961, Robert Gover's *One Hundred
Dollar Misunderstanding*[9] gave prostitution and pornography
a humorous twist. Four years earlier, Hubert Selby, Jr.'s *Last
Exit to Brooklyn*[10] had already given both prostitution and
pornography the benefit of completely unsentimentalized expression. Perhaps a cultural phenomenon has to see itself
clearly before it can laugh at what it imagines that it sees.

Gover's comedy plays on conflicting points of view; Selby's mini-biography of Tralala seems to have no point of view.
Neither treatment could have existed so openly and freely
without the sanctions of both liberalized attitudes toward
obscenity and clinical approaches to intellectual understanding. In Gover one sees a pseudo-intellectual college student
and a streetwise black hooker comment separately on the
same commercial sexual encounter, one that remains, of
course, essentially a misunderstanding. In Selby one sees a
neighborhood prostitute with the neutral objectivity of an all-
seeing clinician. Both writers treat relatively "common" prostitutes uncommonly, and the result is to give both an ironically heroic stature.

Gover's college student rationalizes his visit to a prostitute. "I felt like a detective. . . . I just adopted a very scien-
tifically objective viewpoint" (p. 16). This viewpoint mocks
the stereotype of Charlie's pale cerebral culture itself. In contrast, Kitten is the personification of down-to-earth soul:

> Here goes me, I'm in the big chair. In come this trick by
> hisself. . . . Madam tell this jittery Whiteboy we is all the

cats they is jes now. . . . He so gee-gee jittery an all, she
guess she gonna git his gun wiff out hardly no work. . . .
He dress like he got the jack fer tippin (pp. 19 – 20).

Dialect and detail work together to emphasize or exaggerate
the gap betwen buyer and seller, "old" boy and "old" girl, john
and hooker, white and black.

All literary treatments of prostitution seem suddenly sus-
pect when the self-conscious white hero encounters his and
her own language problems. "This girl (I mean, this professional prostitute). . . . I couldn't understand a word she was
saying. . . . Her entire vocabulary, such as it was, seemed
composed of pornographic slang and insincere endearments"
(pp. 26 – 28).

Economic misunderstandings actually reflect what these
two very different people really have in common, a common
concern that transcends their uncommonly good sex at last.
The white student, roles reversed, prepared his blackmail
scheme to get his money back: "It was time for a showdown,
for the invoking of the law of supply and demand, for the
exercise of the planned and well programmed hard sell" (p.
162). The black woman's coworker also reminds Kitten that
it is time to remember the traditional priorities: "She say,
Kitten ain Madam never tol' you, Jack first, fug secen'?"
(p. 165).

Comedy and realism both know the priorities: Economics is the very common understanding behind the most effec-
tively and uncommonly expressed sexual misunderstandings.
Hubert Selby, Jr.'s *Last Exit to Brooklyn* suggests an even
more common fate and one that may be, at least by implica-
tion, tied to an uncommonly oppressively economic system.

Tralala was 15 the first time she was laid. There was no
real passion. Just diversion. . . . Tralala didn't fuck
around. Nobody likes a cock-teaser. Either you put out or
you don't. . . . She always got something out of it. Theyd

> take her to the movies. Buy cigarettes. Go to a PIZZERIA
> for a pie. There was no end of drunks. Everybody had
> money during the war. The waterfront was filled with
> drunken seamen. And of course the base was filled with
> doggies. And they were always good for a few bucks at
> least. Sometimes more. And Tralala always got her share
> (pp. 95–96).

Such writing, as much as Gover's, represents the prostitute's coming of age in the literature of an age of pornography; it manages sensitivity without moralism or judgment.

> But she got what she wanted. All she had to do was put-
> out. It was kicks too. Sometimes. If not, so what? It made
> no difference. Lay on your back. Or bend over a garbage
> can. Better than working. And its kicks. For a while any-
> way. But time always passes (p. 96).

Gover seems here inside his prostitute even as his commitment to objective acceptance seems neutral at last. One senses a Tralala allowed to be whatever she is and not manipulated to fit a plot of fiction or ploy of self-promotion.

But like the most uncommon of literary prostitutes, Tralala develops. Ambition seems built-in, part of her wartime profiteering social scene.

> But Tralala wanted more than the small share she was
> getting. It was about time she got something on her own.
> If she was going to get laid by a couple of guys for a few
> bucks, she figured it would be smarter to get laid by one
> guy and get it all (p. 97).

The result of Tralala's ambition differs markedly from the results of Adler's and Hollander's.

> 10 or 15 drunks dragged Tralala to a wrecked car in the lot
> on the corner of 57th street and yanked her clothes off and
> pushed her inside and a few guys fought to see who would
> be first and finally a sort of line was formed everyone
> yelling (p. 114).

The end result is as common as it is pornographic: "But they couldn't revive her so they continued to fuck her as she lay unconscious on the seat in the lot and soon they tired of the dead piece and the daisychain brokeup" (p. 116).

The final relationship between prostitution and pornography is a common denominator. Even the most exceptional prostitutes, those whose well-reputed houses reflect American business know-how and success, flirt with violence. Rechy's hustler hero finds on the streets "always a suggestion of violence" (p. 32). Kenrick's *The Chicago Girl* opens with the murder of one prostitute: "She didn't cry out, didn't even put a hand to her face or dart a tongue out to taste the blood. She knew the taste . . . pain, an old and boring acquaintance was back for another visit" (p. 10). Beverly Hills's successful American gigolo is forced, professionally, to inflict pain for money: "The blood, the neurotic hysteria, the incessant commands and instructions were getting on my nerves" (p. 36). Polly Adler's girlhood contained the violent trinity of rape, pregnancy, and abortion (pp. 25 – 26). Joe Buck's teacher and torturer describes the thin line between paid violence and murder: "Marvin can't afford to be murdered, not on his salary. I suppose if he's lucky, somebody might lose control someday and do the thing for free. But not me, I know my work" (p. 53). The violence of *Dressed to Kill* has already resulted in feminist groups picketing the film, which seems to prove the thesis that "love was a perishable commodity" (p. 64). Xaviera Hollander certainly speaks from her own experience and would appear to predict the kind of opposition *Dressed to Kill* has generated when she says, "A man striking a woman . . . is cowardly and animalistic" (p. 65). The college student of *One Hundred Dollar Misunderstanding* finds the reverse cowardly, considering himself "the victim of two ill-repute women who had stooped to using drugs in the lowest possible sort of doublecross" (p. 185).

Contemporary fiction shows the prostitute, male or

female, in the middle of a double-crossed conflict between official and unofficial, respectable and criminal cultures. Hard-boiled moral relativities and hardcore pornography allow and profit by the violent buying and selling of sexual pleasure. Sentimental legacies, the demands of plot, and the egos of writers all stress uncommon characteristics of heroism and realism. The prostitute as an image of the human condition, on her or his experience, can echo Suzie Wong's tentative pessimism: "I don't think people ever got properly cured" (p. 296).

Pornography is essentially violent. Personal characteristics and encounters are wrenched or distorted into impersonal caricatures of themselves. An age of open pornography may make traditional prostitution seem a comparatively personal human relationship, but to repeat Rechy's phrase, there is "always a suggestion of violence" on the street or in the house that is not quite a home. Contemporary American literature is, at last, at least free to express even more than that suggestion of violence with more than common explicitness. But the realistic elements of commercial exchange, the sentimental aspects of golden hearts, and the narrative or personal needs for heroism remain the same as ever.

Women Writing about Prostitutes: Amalia Jamilis and Luisa Valenzuela

AMY KATZ KAMINSKY

PROSTITUTION may or may not be the world's oldest profession, but certainly the prostitute has worked long and hard as one of fiction's most familiar figures. Simone de Beauvoir's analysis of "Myths: Dreams, Fears, Idols" in *The Second Sex* does much to explain why the prostitute has enjoyed such popularity in literature. De Beauvoir recognized that the prostitute, more than any other female figure, exists as a projection of male fantasy. Although men have defined roles and behaviors for all women, those roles are more or less fixed once they are posited. The prostitute, however, is called on to become any feminine type her customer requires.

Thus, men can and have invested the prostitute with all the characteristics they have attributed to women of every sort. Similarly, many writers have used the whore in their works, endowing her with diverse and often contradictory characteristics. Depending on such variables as the writer's background, his or her personal preferences, and the demands of the work, prostitutes in fiction have been depicted as corrupt or pure, wicked or good, victim or seducer, death-dealing or life-affirming.[1] Furthermore, just as male artists have concentrated on the female nude for reasons other than chaste devotion to line, form, and color, male writers often have written painstakingly detailed descriptions of whores with other than purely literary pleasures in mind.

Kessel Schwartz's "The Whorehouse and the Whore in Spanish-American Fiction of the 1960's" offers a veritable catalog of prostitution, beginning with the earliest works by Spanish-American writers.[2] The variety of literary uses to which prostitutes in those works are put confirms the above observations. Yet the picture is incomplete. The authors Schwartz deals with are all men, and the myth of the prostitute de Beauvoir discusses is quite pointedly a creation of the male imagination. In both Schwartz and de Beauvoir, the prostitute is "other," existing only for the man, not at all for herself and hardly at all for other women.

Even among male writers who are sympathetic toward prostitutes, the tendency is to create the character from without, to rely on the role of "prostitute" in defining the character, rather than to seek out the individual in that role. In *Prostibulario*, a collection of Argentinian short stories about prostitutes, all the pieces but one are told from the male point of view. The women in them are of interest only insofar as they relate to a male protagonist or narrator. In only one story are the events seen through the eyes of the prostitute, and that piece is the only one written by a woman.[3]

A single example such as this is not meant to prove anything, but it suggests a great deal. (Among the questions it raises is, Why, despite the large number of women writers in Argentina and the prevalence of the prostitution theme in their work, is only one of the authors represented in the collection a woman?) At the very least, we might begin to consider that women may think and write about prostitutes and prostitution differently from the way men do and that women and men writers create characters who are prostitutes for different reasons. We would do well to pay attention to these women writers if we wish to pretend to something approaching complete understanding of this figure as she is invented in literature. A comprehensive knowledge of the prostitute must include what, and how, the image means for women as well as for men.

Although Spanish-American women writers live in a patriarchal culture and inherit the values and norms of that culture along with its literary tradition, they generally maintain some ties to a female subculture. These ties are reinforced by a system which insists on gender identification and stresses the differences between the sexes. Thus, while women writers may take on some male attitudes when writing about prostitutes (especially when the character is a minor figure), we can assume that a woman writer's approach to her fictional prostitute may well be different from a man's. Although the sort of educated middle- or upper-class Spanish-American woman who is likely to sit down to write a novel or short story is considerably less likely to have had firsthand experience with prostitutes than her male counterpart, her affective ties with them are much stronger than his. When a woman writer confronts the figure of the prostitute, she can see her creation as "other" only on the most superficial level. Given the culture's insistence on identifying "woman" with her sexual function, its association of all female sexual behavior with prostitution, and its tendency to see any woman in the prostitute and the prostitute in any woman, the woman writer in Spanish America soon comes to understand the prostitute not as "other" but as a being somehow connected to herself.

For male writers, the prostitute can embody any aspect of the male-defined feminine. She can be used to illustrate a moral or political lesson, or her sexuality can be used by her creator to appeal to his own and his male reader's prurient interests. For the woman writer, the prostitute serves different purposes. Aron Krich, in his preface to *The Prostitute in Literature*, writes, "If for the man, the prostitute offers an escape from the responsibility of expressing his erotic and affectional needs in a setting of consistent intimacy, for the woman the prostitute becomes an unconsciously unassailable rival, hated but envied and sometimes imitated."[4]

Although we may disagree with Krich's expression of the attitude of other women toward the prostitute and with his implicit placement of the prostitute outside the definition of "person," underlying his statement is the connection between prostitutes and other women. The prostitute represents the idea "woman" carried to the extreme; thus, understanding her means understanding more profoundly the situation of all women. It should not surprise us, as it did Greenwald and Krich, whose book was published in 1960, before the second wave of North American feminism, that they found little information on the subject of the prostitute in literature and that what did exist dated from "the heyday of feminism and the struggle for suffrage."[5] Writers have always created fictional prostitutes; but only recently have critics, enlightened by feminist thought once again, returned to study the phenomenon. Furthermore, we can begin to see that by rescuing the person who is the prostitute, women writers proclaim the similarity as opposed to the otherness of all women.

Luisa Valenzuela and Amalia Jamilis are two among many Argentine women who have used prostitutes as characters in their fiction. Neither calls attention to the universality of her characters' experience; rather, they are primarily interested in creating unique individuals and situations. Yet simply by presenting the prostitutes as complete human beings, Valenzuela and Jamilis require that the reader empathize with their characters.

Clara, the protagonist of Valenzuela's *Hay que sonreír* (literally, *You Have to Smile*),[6] comes to Buenos Aires, becomes a prostitute almost by accident, and finds her freedom eroded as her relationships with men become increasingly formalized. Jamilis's *Los trabajos nocturnos (Nightwork)*[7] is a collection of short stories, some of which are interrelated and tell about an urban commune. The title story does not define the relationships within the commune, nor, as might be expected, is its action central to the lives of most of the characters. "Los trabajos nocturnos," rather, tells about one night in the life of Olimpia, who lives in the commune and works as a prostitute.

By stating that Valenzuela's Clara becomes a prostitute[8] and that Jamilis's Olimpia works as one, I have indirectly raised the question, What does it mean to be a prostitute? This question is not as trivial as it may seem. Once we cut through the rhetoric—all women, or all heterosexual women, or all married women, or all women who have sex outside marriage, or all women who have kissed men good night because they bought them dinner, are whores—we are left only with the sense that prostitution has to do with women and with sex and that it is wrong. (Men can be prostitutes too, of course; but male prostitution is outside the scope of this paper.)

The definition of a prostitute which I will use is the following: She is someone who exchanges sexual services for money, whose clientele is diverse, and who is condemned by society for these transactions. The label "prostitute" is applied by both the individual and the society concurrently. In other words, in order to be a prostitute, a woman must be perceived and perceive herself as one.

Once she has accepted the fact that she is a prostitute—a process which takes a while, since the first time she is given money in return for sex, she consciously avoids saying she earned it, insisting to herself instead that she "obtained" it— Clara remains a prostitute in her own mind only for as long as she continues to work as one. Nevertheless, she remains a whore in the eyes of society until she marries, and she continues to be one forever as far as her husband is concerned. Jamilis's Olimpia becomes a prostitute only when she leaves home for work in the evening, since inside the society of the commune she is accepted and loved. Olimpia is condemned and debased only when she is with a customer or is perceived to be a prostitute by others. When she enters a private drinking club for reasons having nothing to do with sex, she immediately is accosted as a whore. This shocks the reader, because even though Olimpia is dressed for work and looks like a prostitute, the first-person narration leads the reader to think of her as a human being rather than sexual merchandise.

In both *Hay que sonreír* and "Los trabajos nocturnos," there is, then, a discrepancy between self-definition and societal perception, resulting in an ambiguous and difficult situation for the woman. Clara often is reminded that others believe she is a prostitute even when she is not acting as one. This societal apprehension of Clara makes it easy for her to resume her work as a prostitute when she needs money. It also catapults her into marriage. The only way she can rid herself of the stigma of being a prostitute, even though she no longer acts or thinks of herself as one, is by marrying Alejandro. Once she does so, Clara no longer considers resuming her career, though she frequently recalls the comparative freedom and economic independence she had when she was working. As she had expected, Clara gains respectability in the eyes of the world when she marries Alejandro. He, however, continues to think of her as a whore—not a person, but an object he has bought and now owns through marriage, exclusively his and absolutely bound to his will. For Alejandro, the fact that Clara has been a prostitute means that she must continue to be one; the person is subsumed in the role. His view directly contradicts hers, which holds that a woman is a prostitute only when she is making her living as one.

The split between who Olimpia is and what she does is nearly total in "Los trabajos nocturnos." Olimpia is not at all introspective about her work; her humanity is primary, and when it is violated—when she is treated as an object—the reader shares her humiliation.

Clara's longing for respectable domesticity—her devotion to housework when she lives with Victor and her efforts to create a normal home with Alejandro—attests to her sensitivity to what society thinks of her and to how it causes her to perceive herself. Nevertheless, she is not particularly ashamed of or defiant about being a prostitute. Olimpia's feelings about being a prostitute are similar to Clara's. She too is neither ashamed nor defiant, but Olimpia is not in the least inclined toward middle-class values. While Clara looks for happiness in marriage and housewifery, Olimpia chooses to live in a commune with writers, artists, and other marginal folk. While Clara longs for a broom with which to clean Alejandro's apartment and does not dare touch his precious books and artifacts, Olimpia joins in a ritual cleansing bonfire, destroying books and paintings in the commune's courtyard. And while Clara dreams in clichés of home and family, Olimpia's communal family rids itself of its children when they reach the age of three or four.

Other differences between the two are reflected in what the men with whom they live think of these women's prostitution. Yet the differences in attitude among the men are superficial, since they all see the women's actions in terms of themselves and are blind to their meaning for Clara and Olimpia.

Clara's first steady man is Victor. Believing that he has rescued her from a life of degradation and vice, he thinks that Clara owes him eternal gratitude and perpetual maid service. Victor insists that she act the part of the perfect wife, perfectly enslaved and silent. However, since she is not married to Victor, Clara feels free to leave him, which she does, much to Victor's surprise. But Clara is nothing if not honorable and obedient to society's sacred laws. Once she married Alejandro, having promised not to leave him, she feels morally bound to stay. Alejandro is a neurotic bourgeois who is determined to live in squalor. As far as he is concerned, his marriage to a whore is proof of his own degradation. Alejandro enjoys both the abasement he derives from being in contact with her and the absolute power he has over her. Ironically, Alejandro reveals his unreconstructed class affiliation in the very act of acquiring his personal whore, in his attitude toward her, and by insisting for a long time that Clara remain at home and not work, in a grotesque parody of a middle-class marriage.

The men with whom Olimpia lives in the commune are not judgmental of her, as Victor and Alejandro are of Clara. They rather enjoy the idea that Olimpia sleeps with many men; it makes her and them the more exotic. Besides the erotic pleasure Olimpia provides them with by having sex with strangers, the commune's men as well as its women depend on her wages for survival. Unlike Clara, Olimpia does not think of the money she earns as her own. She seems only too eager to get rid of the cash as soon as she arrives home in the morning.

Both Olimpia and Clara work at other jobs related in some way to prostitution. Olimpia is also a stripper, and she occasionally works as a fashion model. The hierarchy of respectability among these three occupations is obvious, but they all have in common the use of one's body for commercial purposes. Clara's second career is as an Aztec flower; she appears as a disembodied head in a carnival. Here, the body's existence is denied by means of an optical illusion, though ironically, Clara's awareness of her body increases as a result of the uncomfortable box into which it is stuffed. It is the deception of the customer who pays for the show that connects Clara's carnival work to her prostitution.

In fiction by men, the fact that a male character has to resort to a prostitute for sexual contact (often confused with love) is usually a sign of his alienation. The prostitute in such cases becomes an incarnation of the devouring mother, a death figure. For Valenzuela and Jamilis, the women themselves, who, by the way, do not confuse sex with love, suffer their own alienation. Olimpia's safety in the bosom of the commune disappears the moment she leaves for work. Furthermore, it is clear that none of her friends, with the likely exception of Nana, a minor character who works with her at the nightclub, knows quite what being a prostitute entails. With her customers, Olimpia is unable to communicate anything about herself at all; since as a whore she is required to conform to their image of her, deny her self, and become whatever they demand she be. Moreover, the men Olimpia meets reveal nothing of themselves, not even their names.

Olimpia is alone in her night world. She has no amulets, no protection. Not even the dress painted for her by her friend Cela is sufficient to defend her against isolation. Yet Olimpia does as she is bidden, with an almost transcendent passivity which also characterizes Clara. In the course of her story, Olimpia is asked to, and does, perform a series of tasks that to her are perfectly meaningless but which put her in danger. All the indignities she suffers—a cut lip, some manhandling, abandonment by a taxi driver—are minor, but all derive from the underlying violence of a malevolent, unpredictable world. Clara, too, becomes trapped in an evil world, but hers is the world her husband creates for her rather than the unknown nightworld of Olimpia. This world of conjugal terror ultimately destroys Clara.

While Olimpia is essentially alone despite her relationships with other members of the commune, Clara's solitude is a direct result of her marriages, imitation and real. Both Victor and Alejandro isolate Clara physically and emotionally. They forbid her to leave the house and deny her economic independence, and each in his own way refuses to communicate with her. Victor talks all the time, never allowing Clara to respond; Alejandro neither talks nor listens. Even Clara's much desired affair with Carlos, which takes place in the context of neither marriage nor prostitution, further alienates Clara, as she learns that Carlos has lied to her and thus cannot be trusted.

Related by a similar process of disillusionment to Clara's alienation is her apparently contradictory desire for freedom and domesticity. Although the prostitute seems to enjoy more freedom than most other women, she is in reality as bound as they, albeit in different ways. While she answers to no one man, the prostitute is dependent on men as a class for her sustenance. Since she is by definition a social outcast, her situation is extremely precarious. Clara arrives in Buenos Aires at the beginning of the novel free of family and responsibility, but she has no money. Under these circumstances, marriage, purported to provide respectability and economic security, seems a haven. However bad Clara's situation is, though, it is immeasurably worsened when she becomes entangled with men.

Two motifs associated with Clara's longing for freedom throughout the work are her desire to see the ocean and her consciousness of an unbound inner world, her ability to imagine and fantasize. She wants desperately to travel to the seaside resort of Mar del Plata, a pitifully short trip but far beyond her means. When she finally gets there, already married to Alejandro, he prevents her from going down to the oceanfront. Valenzuela is not subtle in the symbolism she uses in depicting Clara's marriage to Alejandro. He is a magician in a carnival who hands Clara three fortunes. She chooses one, believing herself to have acted freely because, after all, she has "chosen" her destiny. Even so, she never reads the fortune, never really has her future made explicit. After having kept Clara a virtual prisoner in the house, Alejandro marries her out of fear that some part of her might escape his control if she were to remain legally free. He then takes her inland, increasingly far from the sea, and allows her to leave their quarters only to be crammed into a small box as the Aztec flower. At the end of the novel Clara has no hope of ever escaping Alejandro. Her halfhearted attempt to kill him has failed—she fell asleep, that is, lost control over her thoughts— and in the end it is he who is holding the knife above her throat.

Olimpia also is trapped in her role, though the reader cannot know whether she struggled against her fate as Clara did. The last story in *Los trabajos nocturnos,* called "Los parques cerrados" ("Closed Parks"), serves as an epilogue to the commune sequence. The group has long since disbanded, and all the characters have changed, with the exception of Olimpia. Most of the others appear in their new aspect, but Olimpia does not. We know of her only because one of the others says she thinks Olimpia still works at the nightclub. That is to say that in the end, Olimpia exists only as a memory in the minds of others, never having gone beyond the role of prostitute either in their minds or presumably in her own life.

The shift in narrator from story to story in *Los trabajos nocturnos* creates resonances within the stories and under- scores the discrepancy between the prostitute's reality and a male comprehension of that reality. With the exception of Olimpia, Jamilis's narrators in the commune stories are men, and they reveal a marked emotional distance when speaking of her.[9] This distance is coupled with a morbid fascination with Olimpia's work, which they see as a sort of ancient ritual in which they participate indirectly and through their sexual relations with her.

In reality, Olimpia's working life as she recounts it is quite different. The sexual element is suppressed almost en- tirely; rather than repeating a hazily defined, well-rehearsed ritual, a reenactment of ancient mysteries, Olimpia describes a series of sharply focused, unrelated acts performed for no known reason and in unfamiliar territory. Olimpia's prostitu- tion is related not to primal archetypes and ancient mysteries but to twentieth-century existential anguish.

Valenzuela, like Jamilis, uses multiple points of view, switching from first- to third-person narration. Clara relates her own experiences and thoughts simply but eloquently, and the omniscient speaker with whom she alternates has direct access to Alejandro's consciousness as well. In this way, Valenzuela too takes pains to point out the discrepancy between men's ideas about prostitutes and prostitutes' ideas about themselves.

Certainly one of the major differences between the man's perception of the experience and the prostitute's is the extent to which each believes that the encounter between the prostitute and her client produces pleasure. While it is certainly true that many male novelists are aware that for the prostitute paid sexual encounters are not erotic, there is a strong tendency among them to depict prostitutes for their erotic or even pornographic value. This is understandable if not forgivable, given that from the man's point of view, an experience with a prostitute is expected to produce sexual pleasure. Often, though, the woman is perceived not as an object of pleasure but of disgust. Yet the principle remains the same. It is the man's physical reaction to the woman, either positive or negative, which determines who and what she is.

The prevailing point of view in Jamilis and Valenzuela is the woman's, not the man's. In *Hay que sonreír* and "Los trabajos nocturnos," the encounters between prostitute and client are nonerotic. Indeed, in the short story, Olimpia's interaction with her customer is devoid of sexual content, the better to demonstrate that prostitution is more about humiliation and submission to power than it is about sex. Clara's reactions to sexual contact with her clients range from indifference to mild disgust, though she enjoys having sexual relations with her husband and lover. Although both Clara and Olimpia are described as being beautiful—a device used by men and women alike to signal that these prostitutes are sympathetic characters—neither is described in language which might arouse the reader sexually.

Interestingly, both Jamilis and Valenzuela make a point of mentioning their characters' stupidity. Jamilis undercuts the judgment by putting it in the mouth of a male character who, in a profound way, does not understand Olimpia. Valenzuela likewise mitigates Clara's simplemindedness by making it a part of her innocence, but in both cases the characterization is made. It is there perhaps as a way of permitting a certain dissociation between writer and character or between character and reader, a concession to a society that devalues the prostitute.

This note of self-protection, of conscious anti-identification, is somewhat jarring in light of the respect and compassion Valenzuela and Jamilis demonstrate for Olimpia and Clara. Olimpia's power of observation and Clara's sensitivity belie the assertion that they lack intelligence, yet somehow it is still necessary for "decent" women, writers and readers, to stand aloof from whores.

Notes

THE PROSTITUTE AS SCAPEGOAT: MILDRED ROGERS IN SOMERSET MAUGHAM'S *OF HUMAN BONDAGE*

1. Discussions of *Of Human Bondage* as a *Bildungsroman* include Suzanne Howe, *Wilhelm Meister and his English Kinsmen: Apprentices to Life* (New York: Columbia University Press, 1930), pp. 289–91; Jerome Hamilton Buckley, *Season of Youth: The Bildungsroman from Dickens to Golding* (Cambridge: Harvard University Press, 1974), pp. 249–55; and Robert Lorin Calder, *W. Somerset Maugham and the Quest for Freedom* (Garden City, N.Y.: Doubleday, 1973), pp. 78–130.

2. Annis Pratt in her article "Women and Nature in Modern Fiction," *Contemporary Literature*, 13 (1972), pp. 477, 484, describes Joseph Campbell's delineation of the hero's goal: The "hero comes to 'know' woman and through her the natural world, which the heroine already possesses as an extension of herself. Campbell's hero, perceiving this feminine phenomenon of coextension with nature, uses the woman as a portal through which the green world is perceived." In the male *Bildungsroman*, the quest for reunion with nature through woman results in the progression of the young protagonist from one woman to another until he discovers the one who fulfills his requirement that "his heroine and the green world [be] coextensive parts of each other but rightfully subordinate to him."

3. W. Somerset Maugham, *Of Human Bondage* (New York: Penguin, 1978), p. 598. All subsequent references are to this edition and included in the text.

4. Calder, pp. 107–08, 110–12, demonstrates how the several stages of the Philip-Mildred relationship embody various emotional responses of Philip to Mildred, ranging from humiliation through enslaving emotional bondage and finally pity arrived at through self-analysis.

5. Calder, p. 90.

6. Barbara Fass, *La Belle Dame sans Merci & the Aesthetics of Romanticism* (Detroit: Wayne State University Press, 1974), pp. 20, 22.

7. Calder, p. 111.

8. Northrop Frye, *Anatomy of Criticism* (Princeton: Princeton University Press, 1957), p. 41, discusses this aspect of the scapegoat.

9. Calder, pp. 89–91.

10. Richard Albert Cordell, *Somerset Maugham* (Bloomington: Indiana University Press, 1961), p. 80; Laurence Brander, *Somerset Maugham* (Edinburgh: Oliver & Boyd, 1963), p. 32.

11. Samuel Hynes, *The Edwardian Turn of Mind* (Princeton: Princeton University Press, 1968), pp. 174, 201–06.

12. See Joseph Campbell, *Hero with a Thousand Faces* (1949; reprinted New York and Cleveland: Meridian-World, 1956), pp. 109–16, 302–03. A displacement of the myth of the hero into the realistic *Bildungsroman* finds the young developing protagonist encountering various manifestations of the mother in the ancillary women characters, at least two of whom are often polarized, a reflection of the general tendency in man's art and literature to view woman as either good or evil, angel or witch, helpmate or hindrance, intercessor or seducer. In Victorian fiction, this duality expresses itself in the characters of wife and whore, the latter being either the working-class woman or one fallen from middle-class respectability through sexual indiscretion. *Of Human Bondage* continues the dichotomization into the twentieth century.

13. René Girard, "Violence and Representation in the Mythical Text," *MLN*, 92 (1977), 931, 938, and *passim*.

14. Calder, p. 129.

15. Vivian Gornick, "Woman as Outsider," in *Woman in a Sexist Society*, ed. Vivian Gornick and Barbara K. Moran (New York: Basic Books, 1971), pp. 71–73, 78.

16. Frye, p. 45.

FRENCH FEMINIST THEATER AND THE SUBJECT OF
PROSTITUTION, 1870–1914

1. Maurice Descotes, *Le Public de théâtre et son histoire* (Paris: Presses Universitaires de France, 1964), p. 320. For a general discussion of the representation of women in the French theater from 1850–1870, see Chapter X.

2. Descotes, p. 320. Janin's quotation and all others are translated by me.

3. Mario Praz, *The Romantic Agony*, translated by Angus Davidson (New York: World Publishing, 1956), pp. 108–09.

4. Maria Deraismes, "La Femme dans le théâtre" in *Eve dans l'humanité* (Paris: Sauvaitre, 1891), pp. 102–03. The talk on which this chapter was based was originally given at the Salle des Capucines in 1866. The work *Eve dans l'humanité* is a collection of the talks she gave that year plus subsequent essays.

5. Deraismes, *Eve*, p. 82.

6. Valentine de Saint-Point, "La Femme dans le théâtre," *La Nouvelle Revue*, VIII (1909), 393.

7. Though first published in 1884, Engels's *Origins of the Family* was not translated into French until 1891.

8. The first systematic rebuttal of Proudhon's theories from a feminist point of view was Juliette Lamber's work *Idées proudhonniennes sur*

l'amour, la femme et le mariage, published in 1858. A striking example of reference to Proudhon's theories can be found in Brieux's play *Les Trois Filles de M. Dupont,* in which Julie tells her husband: "On disait jadis de nous: Ménagère *ou* courtisane. Maintenant c'est changé, le progrès a marché—il vous faut les deux dans la même femme: Ménagère *et* courtisane—l'épouse, c'est une maîtresse qui consent à être servante" (III,14).

9. Françoise d'Eaubonne, *Le Féminisme, histoire et actualité* (Paris: Moreau, 1972), p. 120.
10. Jeanne Marni, *Se marier* (Paris: Ollendorff, 1906), p. 227.
11. Eugène Brieux, *Les Trois Filles de M. Dupont,* in *Théâtre complet,* tome 3 (Paris: Stock, 1922), I, 6.
12. Sheila Rowbotham, *Women, Resistance and Revolution: A History of Women and Revolution in the Modern World* (New York: Vintage, 1972), p. 66.
13. Brieux, *Les Avariés,* in *Théâtre complet,* tome 6, III, 5.
14. Gyp, *Autour du mariage* (Paris: Calmann-Lévy, 1883), pp. 94–97.
15. Paul Hervieu, *L'Enigme,* in *Théâtre complet,* tome III (Paris: Fayard, s.d. [1901]), II, 12.
16. Brieux, *Les Trois Filles de M. Dupont.*
17. Brieux, *Les Hannetons,* in *Théâtre complet,* tome 6, II, 5.
18. Brieux, *Les Hannetons.*
19. Brieux, *Les Avariés,* III, 5.

ZOLA'S VIEW OF PROSTITUTION IN *NANA*

1. George Holden, "Introduction" to Penquin edition of *Nana* by Emile Zola (New York: Penguin, 1972), p. 9. Further references will be to this edition by page number in the text.
2. Paul Brulet, *Histoire populaire d'Emile Zola* (Paris: Librairie Mondiale, 1908), pp. 103–04, letter translated by Joanna Richardson in *Zola* (New York: St. Martin's Press, 1978), p. 227.
3. J. G. Patterson, *A Zola Dictionary* (London: Routledge, 1912), p. xiii.
4. Henry James, quoted in Leon Edel, *Henry James, The Master: 1901–1916* (New York: Avon, 1972), pp. 163–64.
5. Translated by Holden, "Introduction" to Penguin edition, p. 11.
6. Zola himself may suggest an example of sublimation, of creative activity in art being similar to and taking the place of the creative act in sex. During years of infrequent sex in his childless marriage to his wife Alexandrine, Zola was a compulsive worker. As biographer F. W. J. Hemmings tells us, "A torrent of inspiration was a positive embarrassment, for then he could not find the words he wanted. ... If he persisted, struggling with a rebellious passage, the effort could actually cause him to have an erection," *The Life and Times of Emile Zola* (New York: Scribner's, 1977), p. 116.

THE MAGIC CIRCLE: THE ROLE OF THE PROSTITUTE IN ISAK DINESEN'S GOTHIC TALES

1. "The Consolatory Tale," in *Winter's Tales* (New York: Random, 1942), pp. 303, 309, 312.
2. "The Old Chevalier," in *Seven Gothic Tales* (New York: Vintage, 1972), p. 103. Hereafter, all quotations are mentioned in parentheses within the text.

THE ROMANTIZATION OF THE PROSTITUTE IN DOSTOEVSKY'S FICTION

1. Donald Fanger, *Dostoevsky and Romantic Realism* (Chicago: University of Chicago Press, 1967), p. 186.
2. Ibid.
3. George Siegel, "The Fallen Woman in 19th Century Russian Literature," *Harvard Slavic Studies*, 5 (1970), 84.
4. Translated by A. C. Coolidge, in *The Harvard Monthly*, 19 (January, 1895), 133.
5. Victor Hugo, *Oeuvres complètes de Victor Hugo*, Vol. III, *Poésie* (Paris: Edition Hetzel-Quantin, 1888), p. 38.
6. Vsevolod Krestovskij, *Sobrani socinenij* (Saint Petersburg: Obscestuennaja Polza, 1899), II, 633.
7. Siegel, p. 93.
8. N. G. Chernyshevsky, *What Is to Be Done?*, translated by Benjamin Tucker (Boston, 1886), p. 164.
9. Viktor Sklovskij, *Za i protiv* (Moskva: Sovetskij pisatel,' 1957), see pp. 125–65.
10. Fyodor Dostoevsky, *Notes from the Underground*, translated by Andrew R. MacAndrew (New York: New American Library, 1961), pp. 185–86.
11. In Edward Wasiolek, *Dostoevsky: The Major Fiction* (Cambridge: M. I. T. Press, 1964), pp. 51–53; and also in Ernest Simmons, *Dostoevsky: The Making of a Novelist* (New York: Vintage Books, 1940), pp. 124–26.
12. Robert Lord, *Dostoevsky: Essays and Perspectives* (Berkeley: University of California Press, 1970), p. 167.
13. Siegel, p. 99.
14. Fyodor Dostoevsky, *Crime and Punishment*, translated by Michael Scammell (New York: Washington Square Press, 1963), p. 192.
15. Simmons, p. 163.
16. Ibid., p. 162.
17. Siegel, p. 99.
18. Fanger, p. 205.

19. George Steiner, *Tolstoy or Dostoevsky?* (New York: Vintage Books, 1961), p. 197.
20. Dostoevsky, *Notes from the Underground*, p. 177.
21. F. M. Dostoevskij, *Pis'ma*, Tom II (Moskva-Leningrad: Gosud. izdat., 1923), p. 169.

THE PROSTITUTE IN ARAB AND NORTH AFRICAN FICTION

1. Albert Memmi, *La Statue de sel* (Paris: Gallimard, 1966), p. 211.
2. Rachid Boudjedra, *La Répudiation* (Paris: Denoël, 1969), p. 23.
3. Naguib Mahfūz, *Qasr al-Shawq* (Cairo: Masr, 1960), p. 396.
4. Jabra Ibrahim Jabra, *Hunters in a Narrow Street* (London: n.p., 1960), p. 45.
5. Assia Djebar, *Les Alouettes naïves* (Paris: Julliard, 1967), p. 423.
6. *The Koran*, "The Believers XXIII," 5 – 6, trans. Arthur J. Arberry (New York: Macmillan, 1970), p. 37.
7. *The Koran*, "The Staircases LXX," 29 – 31, trans. Muhammad Zafrulla Khan (New York: Praeger, 1970), p. 582.
8. Abdelwahab Bouhdiba, *La Sexualité en Islam* (Paris: Presses Universitaires de France, 1975), p. 236.

COURTESANS AND PROSTITUTES IN SOUTH ASIAN LITERATURE

1. J. A. B. Van Buitenen, *Two Plays of Ancient India* (New York: Columbia University Press, 1968), pp. 101 – 05; see also Moti Chandra, *The World of Courtesans*, (Delhi: Vikas, 1973), pp. 134 – 36.
2. Mirza Ruswa, *Umrao Jan Ada/The Courtesan of Lucknow*, translated by Khushwant Singh and M. A. Husaini (Delhi: Hind, n.d.), pp. 10, 12.
3. Ahmed Ali, *Twilight in Delhi* (London: Oxford University Press, 1966), p. 38.
4. R. K. Narayan, *The Guide* (New York: Viking, 1958), p. 73.
5. Mohan Rakesh, *Lingering Shadows,* translated by Jai Ratan (Delhi: Hind, n.d.), p. 74.
6. Bhabani Bhattacharya, *He Who Rides a Tiger* (Delhi: Hind, n.d.), p. 74.
7. Bhabani Bhattacharya, *So Many Hungers* (Bombay: Jaico, 1964), pp. 133 – 34.
8. Khushwant Singh, *Train to Pakistan* (New York: Grove Press, 1961), pp. 25, 26, 28, 31.
9. Yashpal, "One Cigarette," in Corinne Friend, *Short Stories of Yashpal, Author and Patriot* (Philadelphia: University of Pennsylvania Press, 1969), pp. 118 – 19.

10. Manohar Malgonkar, *A Bend in the Ganges* (New York: Viking, 1964).
11. Kamala Markandaya, *Nectar in a Sieve* (New York: New American Library, n.d.), p. 102.

THE FATE OF THE FALLEN WOMAN IN *MAGGIE* AND *SISTER CARRIE*

1. All subsequent quotations are from the Norton Authoritative Text of *Maggie: A Girl of the Streets* (New York, 1979).
2. Introduction to *The Work of Stephen Crane*, Vol. VI (New York, 1926).
3. This and all subsequent quotations are from the Charles E. Merrill Publishing Company facsimile edition of *Sister Carrie* (New York, 1969).

THE UNCOMMON PROSTITUTE: THE CONTEMPORARY IMAGE IN AN AMERICAN AGE OF PORNOGRAPHY

1. Richard Mason, *The World of Suzie Wong* (Cleveland and New York: World Publishing, 1957).
2. Polly Adler, *A House Is Not a Home* (New York: Rinehart, 1953).
3. Xaviera Hollander, with Robin Moore and Yvonne Dunleavy, *The Happy Hooker, My Own Story* (New York: Dell, 1979 [1972]).
4. Tony Kenrick, *The Chicago Girl* (New York: Putnam's, 1976).
5. Brian De Palma and Campbell Black, *Dressed to Kill* (New York: Bantam, 1980).
6. John Rechy, *City of Night* (New York: Ballantine, 1963).
7. James Leo Herlihy, *Midnight Cowboy* (New York: Dell, 1969 [1965]).
8. Timothy Harris, based on a screenplay by Paul Schrader, *American Gigolo* (New York: Dell, 1979).
9. Robert Gover, *One Hundred Dollar Misunderstanding* (New York: Grove, 1961).
10. Hubert Selby, Jr., *Last Exit to Brooklyn* (New York: Grove, 1965 [1957]).

WOMEN WRITING ABOUT PROSTITUTES: AMALIA JAMILIS AND LUISA VALENZUELA

1. Simone de Beauvoir, *The Second Sex*, translated by H. M. Parshley (1951; reprinted New York: Bantam, 1961), pp. 181–82.
2. Kessel Schwartz, "The Whorehouse and the Whore in Spanish-American Fiction of the 1960's," *Journal of Interamerican Studies and World Affairs*, 15 (November, 1973), 472–487.
3. Enrique Amorim et al., *Prostibulario* (Buenos Aires: Merlin, 1967).

4. Harold Greenwald and Aron Krich, *The Prostitute in Literature* (New York: Ballantine, 1960), p. 3.
5. Ibid., p. 1.
6. Luisa Valenzuela, *Hay que sonreír* (Buenos Aires: Americalee, 1966). The novel is available in English in *Clara: Thirteen Short Stories and a Novel,* translated by Hortense Carpentier and J. Jorge Castillo (New York: Harcourt Brace Jovanovich, 1976).
7. Amalia Jamilis, *Los trabajos nocturnos* (Buenos Aires: Centro Editor de America Latina, 1971).
8. Previously, Clara had lived with a pimp who simply exploited her. This male attitude toward prostitution is, perhaps, too uncomplicated to merit inclusion here. Their relationship was brief.
9. There is also a third-person narration which takes the point of view of Misa, a little girl abandoned by the commune. Olimpia is not mentioned in the story.

Notes on the Editors and Contributors

PIERRE L. HORN received his Ph.D. in French from Columbia University in 1974. An associate professor of French at Wright State University, he has published numerous articles on nineteenth- and twentieth-century literature, especially on the image of women in fiction and on women writers of the last twenty-five years. He is now completing a manuscript on Marguerite Yourcenar for Twayne Publishers. In 1978, he was made a Chevalier de l'Ordre des Palmes Académiques by the French government.

MARY BETH PRINGLE holds a Ph.D. in English from the University of Minnesota (1977). She has taught college literature and composition for sixteen years, the last seven at Wright State University, where she is an associate professor of English. A former chairperson of the Women's Caucus for the Modern Languages-Midwest, she has published extensively on women's studies as well as on modern/contemporary literature. Her most recent book is *Sex Roles in Literature*, coedited with Anne Stericker. She is at work now on a study of women's searches for self: "Unsentimental Journeys: Women's Quests in American Literature."

EVELYNE ACCAD teaches French, African, and women's studies at the University of Illinois, Champaign-Urbana. She was born in Beirut, Lebanon, and studied there and in the United States, receiving her doctorate in comparative literature from Indiana University. She has published *Veil of Shame: The Role of Women in the Contemporary Fiction of North Africa and the Arab World; Montjoie Palestine!, or Last Year in Jerusalem;* a short story, "Entre deux" in *Contes et Nouvelles de Langue Française;* several poems in *Mundus Artium* and *Ecriture Française;* and a number of articles and reviews in literary journals.

BONNIE HOOVER BRAENDLIN teaches English at Florida State University in Tallahassee. She has published several articles on the *Bildungsroman* and in women's studies. Currently, she is at work on a study of the Edwardian *Bildungsroman*.

JAMES MICHOS HUGHES is the director of graduate studies in English at Wright State University. An associate professor, he has taught at Wright State since 1964. Hughes has a Ph.D. in American civilization from the University of Pennsylvania (1969). He has published articles on Emily Dickinson, the image of the city, and revolution in literature. His pamphlet on Ohio writer Louis Bromfield appeared in 1980.

LAWRENCE E. HUSSMAN, JR., is a professor and chairman of the Department of English at Wright State University. He received his Ed.D. from the University of Michigan. He has taught at the University of Michigan and the University of Portland and has published on Dreiser and higher education in

America in such journals as *American Literary Realism* and the *Antioch Review.* His book, *Dreiser and His Fiction: A Twentieth Century Quest,* was published by the University of Pennsylvania Press in 1983.

AMY KATZ KAMINSKY has a Ph.D. from the Pennsylvania State University. She is an assistant professor and coordinator of the women's studies minor program of Spanish at the State University College at Oswego, New York. She has published and presented several papers on women writers in Latin America.

AMY MILLSTONE received her Ph.D. in French literature from the University of Wisconsin (1977). After teaching at the College of Wooster and the University of Kansas, she joined the faculty of the University of South Carolina, where she is now an assistant professor of French. Very active in the field of women's studies, she has contributed to an anthology of French language women writers (Stock) and presented a variety of papers on feminism and French women writers. At present, she is preparing a biography of the woman writer and political figure Gyp.

NICHOLAS MORAVCEVICH is a professor of comparative literature, head of the Department of Slavic Languages and Literatures at the University of Illinois at Chicago Circle, and editor of the *Journal of Serbian Studies.* He holds a doctoral degree in comparative literature from the University of Wisconsin (1964) and is the author of a number of articles published in *Comparative Literature, Russian Literature, Comparative Drama, Slavic and East European Journal,* and *Canadian Slavic Papers.*

JILL WARREN is on the staff of the University of California and is currently a writer-editor at Los Alamos National Laboratory. She is a former associate professor of English who has published extensively in the scholarly and popular press. In her spare time, she writes art criticism and does a weekly art review column for the Santa Fe *New Mexican.*

ANN LOWRY WEIR is senior editor at the University of Illinois Press. Her articles on South Asian literature have appeared in the *Journal of South Asian Literature, International Fiction Review,* and elsewhere.

THOMAS WHISSEN was born and raised in Ohio and received his Ph.D. from the University of Cincinnati. He has taught at various schools and universities around the country, including Wright State University, where he is currently a professor of English. He has published extensively in comparative literature and composition. In addition to numerous articles on Isak Dinesen, he is the author of *Isak Dinesen's Aesthetics.* His books on writing include *Components of Composition* and *A Way with Words.*

Selected Bibliography

I. AMERICAN

Crane, Stephen
  Maggie: A Girl of the Streets
  (1893)
Dreiser, Theodore
  Sister Carrie (1900)
Faulkner, William
  Sanctuary (1931)
  The Reivers (1962)
Franklin, Benjamin
  Autobiography (1771–90)
Hawthorne, Nathaniel
  "My Kinsman, Major
  Molineux" (1832)
Jones, James
  From Here to Eternity (1951)
Jong, Erica
  *Fanny: Being the True History
  of the Adventures of Fanny
  Hackabout-Jones* (1980)
Masters, Edgar Lee
  Spoon River Anthology (1914)
Miller, Arthur
  Death of a Salesman (1949)
Miller, Henry
  Tropic of Cancer (1934)
  Tropic of Capricorn (1939)
O'Neill, Eugene
  Anna Christie (1921)
Salinger, J. D.
  The Catcher in the Rye (1951)
Sandburg, Carl
  "Chicago" (1916)
Saroyan, William
  The Time of Your Life (1939)

Slade, Caroline
  The Triumph of Willie Pond
  (1940)
Steinbeck, John
  Cannery Row (1945)
Toomer, Jean
  Cane (1923)
Updike, John
  Rabbit Run (1960)
Wharton, Edith
  House of Mirth (1905)
Whitman, Walt
  "To a Prostitute" (1860)
Williams, Tennessee
  A Streetcar Named Desire
  (1947)
Williams, William Carlos
  Paterson (1951)

II. ENGLISH

Anonymous
  Quem Quaeritis (c. 900)
  "Fair Annie" (c. 1480)
  Mary Magdalene (c. 1480)
Cleland, John
  *Fanny Hill, or Memoirs of a
  Woman of Pleasure* (1748–
  49)
Collins, Wilkie
  The New Magdalen (1872)
Defoe, Daniel
  *The Fortunes & Misfortunes of
  the Famous Moll Flanders*
  (1722)

Roxana, or The Fortunate
  Mistress (1706)
Dekker, Thomas and John
  Webster
  Westward Ho (1604)
Dekker, Thomas and Thomas
  Middletown
  The Honest Whore, Part
  1(1604)
Dekker, Thomas
  The Honest Whore, Part 2
  (1605)
DeQuincey, Thomas
  The Confessions of an English
  Opium-Eater (1822)
Dickens, Charles
  Oliver Twist (1837–38)
  Domby and Son (1847–48)
  David Copperfield (1849–50)
Ford, John
  'Tis Pity She's a Whore
  (c. 1625–33)
Gissing, George
  Unclassed (1884)
Hardy, Thomas
  "The Ruined Maid" (1866)
Joyce, James
  Ulysses (1922)
Maugham, W. Somerset
  Of Human Bondage (1915)
Pinter, Harold
  A Night Out (1960)
Shakespeare, William
  Henry IV, Part 1 (c. 1597)
  Henry IV, Part 2 (c. 1598)
  Henry VI (1599)
  The Merry Wives of Windsor
  (c. 1598–1600)
  Measure for Measure (c. 1604)
  Othello (c. 1604)
  Pericles, Prince of Tyre (c. 1608)
Shaw, George Bernard
  Mrs. Warren's Profession (1894)
Thackeray, William Makepeace
  Vanity Fair (1847–48)

III. FRENCH

Adamov, Arthur
  L'Aveu (1946)
Balzac, Honoré de
  Splendeurs et misères des
  courtisanes (1847)
Baudelaire, Charles
  Les Fleurs du Mal (1857)
Brantôme, Pierre de
  Recueil des Dames galantes
  (1590)
  Recueil des Dames illustres
  (1665–66)
Brieux, Eugène
  Les Avariés (1901)
  Les Hannetons (1906)
Colette
  Chéri (1920)
  La Fin de Chéri (1929)
Dumas fils, Alexandre
  La Dame aux camélias (1852)
Flaubert, Gustave
  L'Education sentimentale (1869)
France, Anatole
  Thaïs (1890)
Genet, Jean
  Le Balcon (1956 and 1960)
Giono, Jean
  Un de Baumugnes (1929)
Goncourt, Edmond de
  La Fille Elisa (1877)
Green, Julien
  Léviathan (1928)
Hugo, Victor
  Marion de Lorme (1831)
  Angélo (1835)
  Les Misérables (1862)
Huysmans, J. K.
  Marthe, histoire d'une fille
  (1876)
Lautréamont, Comte de
  Les Chants de Maldoror (1869)
Maupassant, Guy de
  Boule de suif (1880)

Philippe, Charles-Louis
  Bubu de Montparnasse (1901)
Prévost, Abbé
  Manon Lescaut (1731)
Robbe-Grillet, Alain
  La Maison de rendez-vous
  (1965)
Villon, Francois
  "Ballade de la Belle Heaumière
  aux Filles de Joie" (1462)
Zola, Emile
  Nana (1880)

IV. SPANISH

Arrabal, Fernando
  The Automobile Graveyard
  (1958)
Cela, Camilo José
  The Family of Pascual Duarte
  (1942)
  The Hive (1951)
  Izas, rabizas y colipoterras
  (1964)
  San Camilo, 1936 (1969)
de Rojas, Fernando
  La Celestina (1526, last edition)
Quevedo y Villegas, Francisco de.
  El Buscón (1626)
  Dreams (1627)
Ruiz of Hita, Juan
  Book of Good Love (1330,
  1343)

V. ITALIAN

Boccaccio, Giovanni
  Decameron (1353)
Casanova, Giacomo
  Memoirs (c. 1798; complete
  text, 1960–63)
D'Errico, Ezio
  La Foresta (1959)
Moravia, Alberto
  The Woman of Rome (1947)

VI. SCANDINAVIAN

Bjørnson, Bjørnstjerne
  A Gauntlet (1883)
Borg, Christian
  Albertine (1886)
Dinesen, Isak
  "The Old Chevalier" (1934)
Ibsen, Henrik
  A Doll's House (1879)
Jaeger, Hans
  From the Kristiana-Bohème
  (1885)
Skram, Bertha Amalie
  Constance Ring (1885)

VII. GERMAN

Brecht, Bertolt
  Lux in Tenebris (1919)
  In the Cities' Jungle (1921–24)
  A Man's a Man (1924–26)
  *Rise and Fall of the Town
  Mahagonny* (1927–29)
  The Threepenny Opera (1928)
  *Round Heads and Pointed
  Heads* (1931–34)
  *Mother Courage and her
  Children* (1938–39)
Corrinth, Curt
  Bordello (1920)
Döblin, Alfred
  Berlin Alexanderplatz (1929)
Mann, Heinrich
  *The Goddesses, or the Three
  Novels of the Duchess of
  Assy* (1903)
Von Horváth, Ödön
  Around and about the Congress
  (1929)
  Italian Night (1930)
  Tales from the Vienna Woods
  (1930)
  Kasimir und Karoline (1931)
  Faith, Hope and Charity (1936)
  Pompeji (1937)

Wedekind, Frank
Pandora's Box (1904)
Death and the Devil (1905)

VIII. *RUSSIAN*

Dostoevsky, Fyodor
Notes from the Underground
(1864)
Crime and Punishment
(1865–66)
Gogol, Nikolai
"Nevsky Prospect" (1835)
Tolstoy, Leo
Resurrection (1900)

IX. *ARABO-ISLAMIC*

Boudjedra, Rachid
The Repudiation (1969)
Djebar, Assia
The Naive Larks (1967)
Jabra, Jabra
Hunters in a Narrow Street
(1960)
Khayyám, Omar
The Rubayat (early twelfth
century)
Mahfūz, Naguib
Midāq Alley (1948)
Memmi, Albert
The Salt Statue (1955)

X. *INDIAN*

Ali, Ahmed
Twilight in Delhi (1966)
Bhattacharya, Bhabani
So Many Hungers (1947)
He Who Rides a Tiger (1955)
Kchemendra
Lesson of the Procuress
(eleventh century)
Malgonkar, Manohar
A Bend in the Ganges (1964)
Markandaya, Kamala
Nectar in a Sieve (1954)

Narayan, R. K.
The Guide (1958)
Rakesh, Mohan
Lingering Shadows (1970)
Ruswa, Mirza
The Courtesan of Lucknow
(1905)
Singh, Khushwant
Train to Pakistan (1961)
Súdraka
The Little Clay Cart (c. 500)

XI. *CHINESE*

Kuan Han-Ring
Kieou-fong chen (Yuan Dynasty,
late thirteenth century)
Po Hsing-chen
Li Wa Chuan (Tang Dynasty,
early ninth century)
Tsiang Fang
Ho Siao-yu Chuan (Tang
Dynasty)

XII. *JAPANESE*

Chikamatsu
Love-Suicides at Amijima (1721)
Kafu, Nagai
During the Rains (1931)
Saikaku
*The Life of an Amorous
Woman* (1686)

XIII. *LATIN AMERICAN*

Azuela, Mariano
The Underdogs (1915)
Barrios, Eduardo
Un Perdido (1917)
Gálvez, Manuel
Nacha Regules (1919)
Gambon, Federico
Santa (1903)
García Márquez, Gabriel
One Hundred Years of Solitude
(1967)

Güiraldes, Ricardo
  Don Segundo Sombra (1926)
Jamilis, Amalia
  Nightwork (1971)
Onetti, Juan Carlos
  Junta-Cadáveres (1964)

Valenzuela, Luisa
  *Clara, Thirteen Short Stories
  and a Novel* (1976)
Vargas Llosa, Mario
  The Green House (1966)
  Pantaleon y las visitadorás
  (1973)